The Memoirs of
DENNIS HULL

The Third Best Hull

I SHOULD HAVE BEEN FOURTH BUT THEY WOULDN'T LET MY SISTER MAXINE PLAY

Dennis Hull

WITH ROBERT THOMPSON

ECW PRESS

The publication of *The Third Best Hull* has been generously supported by The Canada Council, the Ontario Arts Council, and the Government of Canada through the Book Publishing Industry Development Program.

CANADIAN CATALOGUING IN PUBLICATION DATA

Hull, Dennis
The third best Hull : I should have been fourth
but they wouldn't let my sister Maxine play

ISBN 1-55022-360-7

1. Hull, Dennis. 2. Hockey players — Canada — Biography.
1. Thompson, Robert, 1971– . 11. Title.

GV848.5.H86A3 1998   796.962 092   C98-931407-3

Design and imaging by ECW Type & Art, Oakville, Ontario.
Printed by AGMV Marquis Imprimeur, Cap-Saint-Ignace, Quebec.
Distributed in Canada by General Distribution Services,
325 Humber College Blvd., Etobicoke, Ontario M9W 7C3.
Distributed in the United States by LPC Group,
1436 West Randolph Street, Chicago, Illinois, U.S.A. 60607.
Published by ECW PRESS,
2120 Queen Street East, Suite 200,
Toronto, Ontario M4E 1E2.

http://www.ecw.ca/press

Contents

Foreword

*I*t's 1964, and training camp for the Chicago Blackhawks has just opened. I'm skating around for a warm-up before our first session began when a black missile, known as a hockey puck, rockets off the glass and careens into the seats with a crash. I turn to see a kid with a mischievous grin. It is my younger brother, Dennis, whom I hardly know.

There is a six-year age difference between Dennis and me. When I left home to embark upon my Junior hockey career, he was a snotty-nosed kid of eight. Four years later I turned pro and went my own way, further separating us.

Our dad kept me up to date on Dennis' hockey career as he followed me to St. Catharines where I played for two years. At that time he had no use for school, and I heard he spent more time as a truant than as a student. But on the ice he was a big, raw, and gangly kid who could shoot the puck a hundred miles an hour.

I vowed I would not try to run his career or private life, but kept a close and wary eye on him. When he would come to me for advice I knew exactly what he needed. Because his name was Hull, the Chicago Blackhawks expected him to play like his big brother, and at times the fans were cruel to him for our differences. But the players knew how valuable Dennis was as a great defensive player and on the road where he was our most consistent winger — a 40-goal scorer playing the same position I did, despite the fact I played 30 minutes or more a game. He had some pretty great stats.

We began to spend more time together socially and I found I had a great kid as a brother — reliable, caring, and very witty. After Dennis retired, a thirst for knowledge led him back to school. He graduated from Brock University with a teaching degree and a major in history, becoming the only one of eleven brothers and sisters to wear the mortarboard. His degree provided him with the tools to teach at the respected Ridley College in St. Catharines. From there he was lured to Chicago, where he became Athletic Director at one of the ten most prestigious technical institutions in the U.S.

A terrific father to his two great kids, John and Martha, and a wonderful husband to Sue, life after hockey flourished for Dennis Hull. He embarked on a speaking career and has blossomed into the greatest after-dinner speaker and master of ceremonies I have ever heard.

Quite a success story: small-town boy makes his dream come true to play in the NHL, graduates from university, teaches at two institutions of note, and becomes one of the most sought-after entertainers in North America!

And one more thing, folks — I'm very proud to be Dennis Hull's older brother!

Love ya, pal!

— BOBBY HULL

ACKNOWLEDGEMENTS

I would like to thank my wife Sue, and my children, John and Martha, as well as Ron Joyce and all the people at Tim Hortons, for the support they've given me during my "third" career. I'd also like to send out a special thank you to Jimmy Pappin and Pit Martin for making me an NHL player. I wouldn't have made it without you!

Thanks to Jack David and ECW PRESS for helping me make this book a reality, and to Ken Walker for suggesting the idea in the first place. I would also like to acknowledge the help Robert Thompson gave me throughout the writing process, Bobby for writing the foreword, and the hard work of my editors, Edna Barker, Jennifer Hale, Andrew Podnieks, and Jeff Davis.

And finally to my partner and best friend Joe Veres, who has made my life in the auto world (at Rose City Dodge in Welland) as exciting as my hockey days.

This book is for all of the people who have seen me speak at banquets across Canada and the U.S. for the last twenty years. I'm sure I'll see some of you again soon.

I found this book most interesting and entertaining, and a true picture of a player I admired so much. Fortunately, my wife Clare and I knew the whole Hull family — Mr. and Mrs. Hull and Dennis's brothers and sisters. Because Clare and I were both from families of eight, we admired the Hull family because of the thoughtful and generous way they were to one another (a gift that many families could use today). I was fortunate to have the great "Golden Jet," Dennis's brother Bobby Hull, play for me. Bobby was the most flamboyant and charismatic player to ever play in the NHL, so when Dennis came along I knew that he would suffer a comparison with Bobby, which he did with the fans in Chicago. Fans are sometimes cruel, but I don't think the fans in Chicago really hated him. They are the best fans in the world.

For a time, Dennis was his own worst enemy. He played great on the road and would stumble over the blue line at home in the stadium. I loved Dennis and felt for him, so much so that I called him into my office and said to him, "Dennis, you are going to be here in Chicago as long as I am, so go out there, relax, and play your game." He certainly did that, and worked hard to become a great left-winger. One thing you can say about Dennis: he was a grumpy guy in the morning, but an absolute joy to be with in the evening.

— BILLY REAY, *former coach of the Chicago Blackhawks*

This book is dedicated to Billy Reay.

ONE

Reaching for the Summit

S ometimes I wonder how I ended up on the ice in Moscow, playing in the most important game in hockey history. I wasn't supposed to be there — it was my brother Bobby who was expected to lead the charge against the Soviets in 1972. But he had chosen to sign with the WHA and wasn't allowed to participate, which left me playing left wing with some of the biggest names in hockey in the most important game ever played. I never considered myself a star, and certainly wasn't in the same league as Stan Mikita, the Blackhawks' legendary centre. But Mikita, who was also on the team, hadn't clicked with the style of play Coach Harry Sinden was implementing, so there I was on the ice while Stan watched the game from a bar in Czechoslovakia.

The series had gone through its distinctive highs and lows, but by the eighth and final game, I knew we could win. The team, which was pared down from its initial 40 players to a more consistent lineup numbering around 20, was playing together as a group. We were united, though things hadn't exactly been smooth.

Before the final game there was already a controversy. Each team had the opportunity to pick the officials for certain games, and in the final it was our choice. The Soviet officials told us the ref we'd picked was sick and that we were going to get Josef Kompalla, a West German referee who had been brutal in the sixth game.

But the team received a boost the day of the game when a telegram, several inches thick, arrived from Canada. It just kept rolling out. Up until that point, we had no sense of our immense Canadian support. The team, after all, had been booed by our own fans following the loss of Game Four in Vancouver. Besides, all we had was Russian television, which seemed to focus on the exploits of Lenin. We knew the games were being televised, but we didn't know the impact they were having in Canada.

In fact, Canada seemed distant when we were in Russia. Moscow itself was the very definition of a culture clash. The first day we walked into Luzhniki Arena, where the Summit Series games were played. There were still construction workers finishing the arena. In the stands a welder was working on something, and I decided to walk over to ask what he was doing. When the shield was flipped up, I realized the welder was a woman. I remember thinking that it was the first time I'd ever seen a female welder.

Likewise, when we'd go into the dressing-room and have a shower, there was a lady who stood nearby and handed out towels. Handing towels to naked hockey players wasn't a big deal to her, as she was obviously in her late sixties or early seventies, but it was really strange to us.

I always dressed beside Pit Martin and Jimmy Pappin before Blackhawks' games. As I got ready for the final, I found myself dressing beside Rod Gilbert and Jean Ratelle, who were my linemates for the final few games. I felt relaxed. I knew I was playing with two great players and we were scoring some goals. On top of that, we felt like a team. However, with the controversy involving the referee, it was clear that the ball was in the Russians' court. At the start of the game, our line assisted on a couple of goals in the first and second periods, but the team found itself down 5–3 heading into the third. The Canadian team had been accused of playing dirty, but in this case the officiating was a problem from the start. Early in the first period, J.P. Parise received a penalty without doing anything to merit one.

"Are you crazy?" J.P. shouted at the ref. "I didn't do anything!"

For arguing the call, Kompalla, the West German ref, gave him 10 minutes more.

"Well, don't bother giving me 10 minutes because I'm going to kill you right now!"

And he broke his stick on the ice and skated at the official as if he was going to whack him over the head. At the last moment, J.P. skated away.

During the intermission before the third period, the Russians put down an inch of water on the ice. There were two Zambonis flooding it, and it's clear the Russians wanted to slow us down. When the buzzer sounded, Harry Sinden told the officials we weren't coming out until the ice froze. We stayed in the dressing room for 10 minutes until the ice began freezing over.

While we were sitting there, Alan Eagleson, the head of the Players' Association, came into our dressing room. The most valuable player of the series was going to get a Ford car, so Eagleson came in and said, "If you guys win this series, everyone will get a new car." (He said it, but after the win the cars never showed up.)

Finally, we went back out on the ice and Esposito scored, putting us within one. Then Cournoyer scored the tying goal, but the goal light didn't come on. Eagleson freaked out.

It must be said that there's no one in the world with a bigger ego than Alan Eagleson, so he must have thought the Russian soldiers who were guarding the ice knew who he was. The Russian crowds were very well behaved, perhaps because the soldiers didn't put up with much. In any case, Eagleson thought he could do things that no one else in the area was allowed to do and when the goal light didn't go on, he ran towards the goal judge. He didn't get far before the guards grabbed him.

The players all went over to where this was happening, but I don't think they had any idea what was going on. The Russian guards couldn't figure out what the big deal was — they were simply dealing with someone who was out of line. But our players rescued Eagleson and took him across the ice before the guards could take him away. In retrospect, we should have let them have him. I admit I wasn't in the group rushing over to help him out — I was lagging behind in the other pack.

After Cournoyer's goal, everything was clicking. Our goalie, Ken Dryden, had the Russians figured out and was playing back in the net, where he was better able to pick out the shots the Soviets took from close range. Phil Esposito was playing well, and Paul Henderson was playing better than he had at any time in his career. But the game was nearing its end and we were only tied.

I was on the ice when, with two minutes to go, there was a break for a television commercial. The Russians seemed confused by it, but Ford and Labatt's had paid a lot of money and they had already lost a lot of money because sometimes the ref would ignore the commercial and drop the puck anyway.

During this break I looked up and saw that Leonid Brezhnev, the head of the Russian government, was sitting above the ice in a box. The whole politburo was there, as well. They were facing the ice, but people in the seats couldn't see them.

Despite the game being tied, Brezhnev was kissing the other Russian politicians on the cheek as a sign of celebration because a tie would give the Russians a win in the series. The Russians had put more pucks in our net at that point and, in the event of a tie, the number of goals would decide the series.

I played 20 more seconds and then the Russians changed and we went off. Peter Mahovlich and Phil Esposito and Yvan Cournoyer came on with a minute to go, and soon after Peter hit the ice, Paul Henderson stood up on the bench and yelled at Peter to come off. Esposito was finishing the game because that's who we wanted out on the ice. It's a famous scene now where Henderson took a shot, fell behind the net and got up just as Esposito passed the puck at an awkward angle. It was a sweeping pass towards the net and Henderson got his stick on it. He was initially stopped, but on the rebound he pushed the puck past the Soviet goalie, Vladislav Tretiak.

I can't understand why Tretiak didn't stop it. Henderson came out in front of the net and simply banged it, and in it went. It was a goal that I felt Tretiak should have had. Even when I see replays today, the goal doesn't look normal. It was so strange that even when we tried to recreate it in the twenty-fifth reunion, we had to do it seven times before we could get it right.

After Henderson scored, the whole team jumped out on the ice, but the game wasn't over and Harry knew it. There were still 34 seconds remaining, but the Russians never really tried after Paul scored. They were finished. They didn't pull the goalie, they didn't rush, they didn't give it all their effort.

I'm not sure whether — at that time — Henderson realized the magnitude of his goal. I often wonder why he couldn't keep that level of play going throughout his career. Maybe he was successful in the series because he was playing with Bobby Clarke at centre, something which worked well for him.

He became a born-again Christian soon after the series and still says he thinks he was put on this earth just to score that goal, which led him to finding God. If that's the impact the goal was going to have on the scorer, well, I'll tell you that I wake up every day and thank my lucky stars that it wasn't me that scored.

When we came off the ice, Cournoyer was sitting next to me and I asked him if this was like winning the Stanley Cup, especially considering that Cournoyer had played on the Montreal team that had beaten the Blackhawks for the Cup the previous spring.

"No, Dennis — this is 10 times better!"

From that point on, despite the fact I never managed to play on the top team in the NHL, I've always felt like I've won ten Stanley Cups.

TWO

Bobby's Little Brother

*I*t wasn't until I went to St. Catharines in 1960 that being Bobby Hull's younger brother struck me as being a challenge. Growing up, it had always been fun to be known as his brother, especially since, right from the start, Bobby was a great player. He was so big and muscular for his age that he dominated the games he played in Belleville, the town near our home where every one of the boys in my family played hockey. In 1952, by the time Bobby was 13, he was already on his way to stardom, off to play his style of fast, flashy hockey in Hespeler, Ontario, for one of the Chicago Blackhawks' farm teams. From there he went to nearby Woodstock where his team won the Ontario championship and then to St. Catharines, one rung on the ladder down from the Blackhawks and the NHL. But the NHL beckoned and in 1957–58, Bobby scored 13 goals for the Blackhawks in his first season with the team. It had taken him five years from when he left Pointe Anne, our hometown on Lake Ontario, to play in the NHL.

I was never jealous of my brother, even later when I began to hear the people compare me to him, often in unflattering terms. I was eight when Bobby started with the Blackhawks and it was certainly exciting to hear the stories about him that floated around town. When you come from a family of 11, there is no jealousy. The Hulls simply didn't function that way. For years I'd slept in the same bed as my brothers. In fact, Bobby says he never slept alone till he got married.

If anything, the esteem in which I held my brother got me in trouble. When you're young and your brother has left home to play hockey, well, it makes you a bit of a hero. I revelled in the fact I was the brother of Bobby. Though not as flashy a player as Bobby, I stood out in Pee Wee and regularly scored a lot of goals. At the time there was an all-star team picked from the ten teams in the area, and it looked very much like I'd make the team. The all-star game was played in Kingston, some 30 miles from Pointe Anne. Everyone expected I was a sure choice, except I didn't make the team.

"Why didn't Dennis get picked for the team?" one of my friends asked the coach.

"Because he talks too much about his brother," was the response.

But by the time I reached Junior, I was at an age where I wanted to be known for my accomplishments. I loved my brother and never held the comparison against him. It wasn't his fault. It's just that the comparison was so easy. We looked alike, we both played left-wing, we had a similar skating style, and we both had a big slap shot.

Bobby, though, always had the great shot. As long as I can remember, he could always do it. I wasn't blessed in the same way Bobby was, but by the time I was 12, I wanted a great shot too.

The Canadiens, the Montreal Canadiens' farm team, used to play against the Belleville McFarland-Juniors in the senior league games, and since Belleville wasn't far away, we'd often go to see the McFarlands play. There was a kid on the Canadiens named Bobby Rousseau, who was 18 at the time, and could slap it from the blueline. I remember being amazed that someone could actually do that.

I wanted to have a shot as good as Rousseau's, so I practised all summer to develop the skill needed. I'd get a piece of linoleum and put it on a road that ran down to the factory. About 60 feet from the road there was a garage, and I'd take the linoleum, lay it down and shoot at the garage, which was made of concrete, like everything else in a town that was built around a cement factory. I'd shoot the puck and then I'd walk up to the garage, pick the puck up, turn around and walk back to the garage. Because I only had one puck, I'd shoot it for hours and hours, but it took a while to walk up to the garage and bring the puck back. But the work eventually paid off. The difference between Bobby's shot and my shot was obvious though. Bobby could shoot a puck through a car wash without it getting wet. I couldn't hit the car wash.

People used to say, "It must be genetic, something with those Hulls." But it's just practice — I simply wanted to have a good shot and worked for hours to develop it. Once Bobby made the NHL, he'd give me these fabulous Northland sticks he used that had "HULL" printed on them. I continued to practise using these sticks.

With Brett (Bobby's son) playing now, the theory of the Hull shot being in our genes has emerged again. There's a right-winger who plays for the Florida Panthers named Jody Hull, who isn't a relation. The night they retired Bobby's number in Winnipeg, Brett had a day off, so he and I flew up to Winnipeg. The club retired Bobby's number before the game in an amazing ceremony. After that, the Jets played Hartford, the team Jody Hull was skating for at the time. Brett and I were watching the game, and Hull got a breakaway and wound up for the big blast. The only problem was that he shot it about 40 miles an hour, as opposed to the 100 miles an hour that Bobby's shot was clocked at.

Brett looked perplexed.

"Uncle Dennis, I think either he's got to improve his shot," Brett said, "or change his name."

*T*he shot aside, comparing me to my brother wasn't fair. From the start it was clear that Bobby was special. The media coverage Bobby received while he was growing up was like the coverage Wayne Gretzky received when he was in his early teens living in Brantford. Though Pointe Anne, a company town on the Bay of Quinte, wasn't exactly the most obvious place to develop a great hockey star, everyone in the area knew about Bobby and followed his every move.

It's funny, but Bobby, from a very young age, was always treated differently by those around him. When he was 12 years old, he was playing Bantam. My dad always made him play a league up, saying to Bobby that it was better for his game.

"Just because you're better than *those* kids, you're not going to get better unless you play against someone older," Dad told him.

I know the lecture: it's one I heard when I started playing against boys who weren't my age. On this occasion I was sitting with my mother watching him play. After the game was over, we sat with Bobby and began watching the next game. All of a sudden this kid came up into the stands with his father.

"This kid is going to be a great hockey player," I heard the father say. "Go up there and get his autograph."

The child, who wasn't much younger than Bobby, looked a little confused by the situation, but did what his father said and came up to him in the stands.

"Robert, can I have your autograph?"

Bobby turned to my mother and said, "Mom, what's an autograph?"

"Robert, this boy thinks you're a special player and he wants you to sign your name so that if you become an NHL player, he can say he met you," Mom explained. Bobby signed his name for the boy, who left the stands and went on his way. But Mom wasn't finished.

"If you do become an NHL player and kids ask you for your autograph, never turn them down."

He never did.

Bobby's notoriety continued in the area even after he'd left and had begun his career in the NHL. In the late fifties, the sports broadcaster on the station from Kingston was Max Jackson. The whole family would always gather around the TV to see how Bobby had played, and sometimes, at the end of the night, he'd say, "Mrs. Hull, Bobby scored," right on the TV, which was pretty exciting when you're 11 years old.

I remember going to see him play in Hespeler. Everybody thought he was going to be a great star and was excited about following his career. But when you're his brother, it was a different story. It was beyond exciting; it was simply amazing to see him play. When Bobby was playing Junior, my mom and dad would occasionally go to see him play in Toronto or Guelph. The drive took many hours because Dad drove a Model A Ford, not the fastest of cars. A few times they even saw Bobby play afternoon games in Maple Leaf Gardens.

But there were 10 Hulls in the family after Bobby left, and Dad drove an antiquated car, so only two of us, Mom and Dad aside, could ever go to see him play. The chance of it happening was the equivalent of winning a lottery.

I remember an occasion when they went to Peterborough to watch Bobby play and it wasn't my turn to go. As the time to leave approached, I got into the back seat of the Model A. It was four in the afternoon and I knew the car wouldn't be leaving until five, so I crouched down to avoid being seen. Mom and Dad got in the front seat and I was lying on the floor when my brothers Ron and Garry got in. They were both a couple of years older than I was, and knew how much I wanted to go. They didn't give me away. I stayed on the floor until we were too far from home to turn back. Everyone was talking and eventually I started talking as well. And, as the conversation progressed, my dad began talking to me. Then, quite suddenly, he stopped.

"What the hell are you doing here?" he roared.

*N*eedless to say, Bobby was a hard act to follow. By the time
I hit my teens, I had developed as a player and wanted to
be known for something other than being the younger brother of
one of the best players in hockey. I wanted to be known as Dennis
Hull, a good hockey player in my own right, but I always got the
same response from people who saw me play: "Hey, that's Bobby
Hull's brother." But there I was, in my first year away from home,
playing the game I loved and set back by a comparison that was
unfair to a teenager of 14.

It was something that bothered me throughout my early
hockey years. I hated it, in fact. Time and again, I was compared
to Bobby by hockey people who should have known better. I
scored 48 goals in Junior, after all, but the coverage was always
the same: Bobby Hull's brother scored a goal last night. Not
Dennis Hull scored, but Bobby Hull's brother scored.

Of course I should have known that following Bobby was going
to be difficult. He had revolutionized hockey, taken it, single-
handedly in my opinion, from a defensive game and changed it
into the fast-paced, offensive style that is played today. It's
Bobby's legacy to modern hockey.

Comparing my play to Bobby's really bothered me when I was
in Junior, but once I got to Chicago, it wasn't as big a concern. I
was just Bobby Hull's teammate. In fact, everyone was known
simply as Bobby Hull's teammate because not only was he better
than me, he was also better than everyone else.

THREE

Those Goddamn Hulls

For the whole family, hockey was the most important thing in our lives. My mother watched and my father played senior and coached. In fact, he met my mother at a hockey game. She went to see a game he played in and someone introduced them. He was quite a hockey player, and was still playing when I was nine or 10. In fact, the first time Bobby's picture was in the paper was when he played on a line with my dad and my brother-in-law. Bobby was 13.

There is a little bay off the Bay of Quinte, and 100 yards off shore, and as soon as it froze over, we'd start playing. I only had two sisters who were younger, since almost everyone was older. My sisters would play, and when I got older, Bobby and I would play against my other two brothers.

I wore my sisters' skates, actually. We used to get hand-me-downs and seeing as I had seven sisters, I'd get their skates. My sisters were all good players. In fact, my dad said my sister Maxine was the best out of all of us. The problem was that she couldn't find a team that would let her play. It was 1950, and since I was five at the time, I didn't know there was anything unusual about wearing girl's skates — or clothes for that matter. It was only when I was playing minor hockey in Belleville and some kid said to me, "Hey, you got your sister's coat on." And I said, "How do you know it was my sister's coat?" And he said, "'Cause it buttons the other way." And when I got my first coat, I still tried to button it the other way.

We'd go down and clean off the snow for a game, and in a little town of 250, everybody's house was near the water. So we'd be shovelling it and marking it off so it was NHL-size. We spent hours cleaning it off and all of a sudden there were enough guys for two teams. I always thought they were watching through their windows, waiting for the stupid Hulls to come and clear off the ice and then they'd come and play.

Of the Hull boys, there were always defining traits. Bobby was always big for his age, and Garry was noted for his white hair. For obvious reasons, everyone called him "Whitey." Soon that was the only name I used in relation to him. It was always Whitey. We are two years apart in age, and when I was five, Dad took us to the circus under a big tent. We were sitting by the stands and were right near the spot where the midgets came in. When they entered, they stood in the aisle and waited for their turn. Garry and I leaned over the railing in front of us to get a good look at them, and one of the midgets noticed us.

"Hello there, Whitey," the midget said.

I turned to Dad, stunned by what had just taken place.

"Dad," I said, "the midgets know Whitey, too."

My dad told that story for years.

Once we started playing organized hockey, we had to go to Belleville, which was seven miles away. The younger you were, the earlier you had to play, which meant most of my games were played around 6 AM. So for someone from out of town, the question was how to get there without a ride? We used to have a bus service and my brothers Garry or Ron would go with me sometimes because their games often followed mine. Bill Akey was the bus driver's name, and God did he hate the Hulls. His bus would go at 6 AM if there was anyone who had to go and if there was nobody to go, he wouldn't take the bus out.

So Saturday morning, nobody ever went, except the Hulls. The kids in our town wouldn't even get up to play, and we were just amazed that they didn't want to play organized hockey. Garry was very mechanical and he seemingly could do anything with machines, including stealing my dad's car when he went away. Often when we went to Akey's place it would be -30°C and Garry would cross the wires and start the bus. Then we'd go wake up Bill Akey.

He'd always say, "You goddamn Hulls! You rotten bastards!" He'd have to get out of bed and drive us to Belleville; then we'd play and get ready for the run back to Pointe Anne. It would be noon and we'd get to the bus station and he'd be sleeping in the back. We'd have to wake him up again to take us home. God, how he hated us.

Since there was nobody really going on that 6 AM run, he eventually cancelled it. It was the only way he could get rid of us. My dad would have to drive me because my mom didn't have a licence. When my dad worked midnight to 8 AM, there was no way for me to get to Belleville. On a couple of occasions, I had to walk. I lived my whole early life waiting for Saturday — the only thing that I dreamed about was playing that half hour. Everything was predicated on me playing on Saturday. Garry and I would play on the outdoor rink until 2 AM and then get up and go to school. But everything was geared towards that Saturday morning. On a couple of occasions, when I was 11 years old, my mother got me up, made breakfast, and sent me out the door. I then walked the seven miles. And that was with my equipment on, instead of carrying it. It was a little scary. From the little town of Pointe Anne out to Highway 2, it was about two miles. And there was nothing there. No houses. Then I'd get to the highway and I'd walk the rest of the way into Belleville. Occasionally a car would come by and I'd get a ride, but a number of times I walked all the way into town.

I tell my son that and he says, "Dad, you're stupid." But he doesn't understand how important it was to me. My mother understood. How many mothers would let their 11-year-old walk all that way on their own? Just to play the game and maybe get your name in the paper — that was my whole life.

Dad

*I*t's strange, but for a small town of only 250 people, 13 of whom were Hulls, Pointe Anne had a number of people who became well known.

There was Manley McDonald, who became a respected painter (one of his pictures hangs in Buckingham Palace), and Murny Carter, a race boat driver who built his own Canada 1 class boats. He was the world champion when I was a kid, which was a pretty big deal. Boat racing sort of became the town's official sport.

On Dominion Day, the first of July, the company would bring in boats for a race. On the lake was a log raft that, for the most part, was used as a platform for the kids to jump off. On this occasion, the raft was towed out to where the boat races would be held. The officials on the raft had a shotgun, which was used to start the race, and the cashbox, which held the prize money. As soon as a boat won, men from the company would pay them right from the raft.

The raft was two-tiered and people would often climb up to the second level. But, on this occasion, as more and more people got up on the second level, the raft became unbalanced and tipped. The spectators crashed into the water along with the shotgun and the cashbox. Then, as if it had never happened, the raft bobbed back right side up.

The officials didn't let the accident slow down the races, and someone was dispatched to get another cashbox and gun.

However, after the races were over, the kids from the town decided to try to get the box and the gun, which were sitting in about 30 feet of water. My brothers and I took a little boat I had, rowed out to the spot where the box and gun had gone down and dove in. But just as you got to the bottom, you had to come right back up. I went home and Dad said, "Did you get any of that stuff that came off the raft?"

"No," I told him. "I could just get to the bottom."

"Goddamn it, you guys are useless," he said.

He went and got his bathing suit, which was made of wool, with a belt on it. He put it on and it had a hole in the back where a moth had eaten through it. He got in the back of this big boat that was used for fishing in Point Anne and he rowed it out.

When we got out there, he spent some time examining the area and figuring out just how the cash box had gone down and how it would float due to the current.

"Stop right here!" he said to me and he rolled over the back. He was a great big guy, probably around 260 pounds at the time and he went straight for the bottom. I thought he'd come up for air, but I could see him, and he didn't surface for what seemed like minutes. I was pretty sure he was finished and I began to think of how I'd explain it — "Well, he was diving in to get the cash box, see" — when all of a sudden he surfaced with the cash box in one hand. He put it in the boat, dived out again and moments later came up with the gun.

In a small town there are always stories of things that become almost myth-like, and in Pointe Anne, Dad was often at the centre of them. One story that got passed around was about how he swam underneath a cement carrier that was docked outside the plant. The carrier was filled with cement and was around 120 feet long and about 60 feet wide. When it was loaded, it drafted

25 feet and that was the lowest it could go, because the Bay of Quinte was, at its deepest, about 30 feet deep.

My father, who could never resist a challenge, dived into the water with one of his co-workers and soon afterwards surfaced on the other side of the boat. It was big news, but I don't think Dad was all that impressed with himself.

"I've done a lot of stupid things in my life," he said. "But when I was underneath the keel, in the middle, I was running out of air. And I knew I had to still go up and in the last ten feet I was sucking in water."

*M*y father was certainly a tough guy. He'd started at Canada Cement when he was 13 and he retired after 47 years when the company moved the plant in 1980. In Pointe Anne, life always revolved around the factory. Everyone worked there, the noise was always there and you just got used to it.

I remember dozens of times when Dad would be sleeping and then suddenly something would happen at the plant, which would wake him up.

"I gotta go to work," he'd say. "The kiln's down."

Hockey and his family aside, that factory was his life.

Even though I was the youngest, he was as tough on me as he'd been on my older brothers. Maybe that's why Bobby and I made it while other talented kids didn't.

One day he was taking Garry, Ron, and Bobby to play in Belleville and I tagged along. It was really icy and when we were about a mile away from the rink, the Model A slid and smacked right into the back of a bus. Everyone stopped and we got out of the back seat of the car and started running for the arena, which wasn't far away.

"Get back here, you bastards!" he yelled at us as we were running down the road, away from the accident.

"Even that little brat is leaving me," he said as I ran towards the arena.

He always claimed he wore out three cars driving us around, but I only remember the Model A.

$\mathcal{W}$ hen Bobby was in the NHL in 1960, Don Murphy, who was the PR director for the Blackhawks, coined the phrase "the Golden Jet" as his nickname. At one point or another that year, the fact the announcers were calling Bobby by his nickname hit my dad while we were watching the Blackhawks play.

"Hey, look at your brother, they're starting to call him the Golden Jet."

"That's a great name," I said. "Think of the way he skates and his blonde hair. That's a great name."

"Ah, big deal," came the response.

"Well, did you have a nickname when you played?" I asked.

"Yeah, the Blonde Flash."

"Really? Who gave you that name?"

"I did," he replied.

He even had his own claim to fame, which he'd tell me time and again.

"I can squat lower, jump higher, dive deeper, stay under longer, and come up drier than any son of a bitch alive," he'd proclaim.

"But Dad, do you think you can make any money out of that?" I'd always ask him.

It's funny, though, because money wasn't Dad's prime concern when Bobby signed with the Blackhawks. It was playing time. In the fifties, there was no entry draft. The way it worked was NHL teams sponsored Junior teams in different towns. If they sponsored the team, then they had the right of first refusal for any player who played on that team. It was like indentured servitude, in a way, but that's the way it was.

Every team came to our house asking Bobby to play for them. The Montreal Canadiens' chief scout came, as did players from Detroit, like John Wilson. I remember being amazed by the fact a Red Wing was in our house. They offered Bobby jackets and other incentives to play. Everyone wanted him, but Dad had a peculiar way of finally deciding where Bobby was going.

He chose the Blackhawks because they were in last place.

"Those guys aren't any damn good," he'd say to Bobby. "The only chance you've got of making the NHL is with these losers."

○

*H*e was a good hockey player in his time, I'm told, and I can still remember watching him play when I was nine or ten. Bobby, my brother-in-law Ray Brannigan, and my dad were on a team in the Trent Valley league. My dad played centre, Bobby played left wing, and Ray played right wing. I was the stick boy. It was around this time that I first remember hearing Dad swear. Dad's team was playing in Tweed, a small town north of Belleville.

The bench in the old arena was down near the goal line and the staff used a fire hose to flood the ice between periods. The problem was that when the ice was watered down, they'd hit the net which would freeze because it was well below zero in the arena. Add to this the fact that when you played a game on the road, your team would only get credit for a goal if the puck went into the net and actually stayed there. Then the goal would be indisputable. If the puck went in and bounced out, the home team would never count it.

During this game in Tweed, my dad was going down the ice and passed it to Ray, whom we called Shanty. Shanty shot the puck into the net and it came out. The goal judge refused to call it a goal. Right away, Dad was behind the net yelling at the goal judge.

"You blind son of a bitch!" he screamed. "You rotten bastard!"

"No goal," the judge said.

A little while later, Bobby shot the puck and it went in the net and out. But it wasn't called a goal, which made Dad even more livid. He called the goal judge every name in the book. In the third period, Ray had the puck coming across the blueline and Dad began yelling for the puck. Ray gave it to him in the slot and my old man fired it and the net simply blew apart. The puck went right through it.

And he went around behind the net and looked right at the goal judge.

"Count that one, cocksucker," he said.

*T*he first time I saw Bobby play for the Blackhawks was in Montreal against the Canadiens. My dad loved to go to the games because he basked in the fame of being Bobby Hull's father. We'd sit in the lobby of the Mount Royal Hotel, where the Blackhawks used to stay, and wait for Bobby to come down and go to the game. While killing time, Dad would talk hockey with anyone who'd listen. Sometimes it was the media, sometimes fans, sometimes other players. He'd loudly tell stories about hockey and Bobby to anyone who cared to listen. He had an opinion on anything. But being so loud got him in trouble from time to time. When you come in to the Mount Royal, there are steps off the street, and I remember seeing a German Shepherd coming in ahead of us.

"Look at that son of a bitch bringing that dog into this nice hotel," Dad said loudly.

But as we got closer, we could see it was a blind guy.

"Oh, the poor bastard's blind," Dad said, equally loudly.

"Yeah Dad, but he's not deaf," I muttered.

Later we were heading to the game at the Forum in a cab. We got to the entrance of the Forum on Rue de Maisonneuve and Bobby said, "Dad, the street's one way, so don't get out on that side, get out on the curb side."

BILLY REAY

Hockey Career

1932 - 1977   45 Years

*Championship Teams **
First Place Teams   *

1932-33	East Kildonan Bisons - Manitoba Midget League - Joe Mathewson, Coach.
1933-34	East Kildonan Bisons - Manitoba Midget League - Joe Mathewson, Coach.
1934-35	Elmwood Maple Leafs - Manitoba Juvenile League - Bob O'Dowda, Coach.
1935-36	Elmwood Maple Leafs - Manitoba Juvenile League - Bob O'Dowda, Coach.
*1936-37 *	St. Boniface Seals - Manitoba Junior League - Geo Browns, Coach. We were defeated in Manitoba Finals by Wpg. Monarchs , who then won the Memorial Cup.
*1937-38 **	St. Boniface Seals - won Memorial Cup - emblamatic of Jr. Championship of Canada.
1938-39	Calgary Stampeders - Alberta Senior Hockey League - Dave Duchak, Coach.
1939-40	Omaha Knights (professional) - American Ass. Hockey League - Rookie of the year "Hap" Emms, Coach.
1940-41	Omaha Knights - we were defeated in finals. "Hap" Emms, Coach.
1941-42	1/2 season coach Sydney Millionaires - Cade Breton Senior League
1942	Married on April 26th to Clare Toronto, Ontario.
*1942-43 **	Coached Morton Aces to Eastern Canada Intermediate Championship.
1942-43	Quebec Aces - Quebec Senior Hockey League - lost in finals - Don Pennison, Coach.
1943	Daughter, Adele Louis Reay born August 27, 1943.
*1943-44 **	Quebec Aces - Quebec Senior Hockey League - Coached and played - won Allan Cup - emblamatic of Senior Championship of Canada.
1944-45	Quebec Aces - repeated as champions with myself as playing coach and manager. I also won the scoring championship plus the Lady Byng Trophy as most gentlemanly player plus all star center.
*1945-46 **	Montreal Canadians - NHL - 1st place finish, won Stanley Cup (player) Dick Irvin, Coach.
*1946-47	Montreal Canadians - NHL - 1st place finish Dick Irvin, Coach.
1947-48 *	Montreal Canadians - NHL - 5th place finish Dick Irvin, Coach.
1948-49	Montreal Canadians - NHL - 3rd place finish (assistant captain) Dick Irvin, Coach.
1949-50	Montreal Canadians - NHL - 2nd place finish (assistant captain) Dick Irvin, Coach.
1950-51	Montreal Canadians - NHL - 3rd place finish (assistant captain) Dick Irvin, Coach.
*	This year while playing for the Canadians, I also helped Sam Pollock coach the Junior Canadians to the Memorial Cup - Junior Championship of Canada.
1951-52	Montreal Canadians - NHL - 2nd place finish (assistant captain) player, Dick Irvin, Coach. Son, William Albert Reay born March 5, 1952.
*1952-53 *	Montreal Canadians - NHL - 2nd place finish won Stanley Cup, Dick Irvin, Coach.
1953-54	Victoria Cougars - Playing Coach - Western Pro Hockey League
1955-56	Victoria Cougars - Playing Coach - Western Pro Hockey League, lost in Semi-Finals
1956-57	Rochester Americans - AHL - Coach, lost in finals
1957-58	Toronto Maple Leafs - NHL - Coach.

Billy's long career and 542 victories as a coach should put
him where he deserves to be: in the Hockey Hall of Fame.

Page 2

1958-59	Toronto Maple Leafs - NHL - Coach (1/2 season)
*1959-59	Belliville MacFarlands - Manager - World Hockey Champions, won in Prague, Czek.
1959-60	Saule Ste Marie Greyhounds - Coach - E.P.H.L. lost in finals.
1960-61	Buffalo Bisons - AHL - Coach.
**1961-62	Buffalo Bisons - AHL - Coach won Calder Cup (emblamatic of American Hockey League)
1962-63	Out of Hockey - worked for Toronto Telegram Newspaper
1963-64	Chicago Blackhawks - NHL - Coach 2nd place finish.
1964-65	Chicago Blackhawks - NHL - Coach 3rd place finish.
1965-66	Chicago Blackhawks - NHL - Coach 2nd place finish.
*1966-67	Chicago Blackhawks - NHL - Coach 1st place finish (first team in Blackhawk history to finish in first place.)
1967-68	Chicago Blackhawks - NHL - Coach 4th place finish.
1968-69	Chicago Blackhawks - NHL - Coach 6th place finish.
*1969-70	Chicago Blackhawks - NHL - Coach 1st place finish.
*1970-71	Chicago Blackhawks - NHL - Coach 1st place finish.
*1971-72	Chicago Blackhawks - NHL - Coach 1st place finish.
*1972-73	Chicago Blackhawks - NHL - Coach 1st place finish.
1973-74	Chicago Blackhawks - NHL - Coach 2nd place finish.
1974-75	Chicago Blackhawks - NHL - Coach 3rd place finish.
*1975-76	Chicago Blackhawks - NHL - Coach 1st place finish.
1976-77	Chicago Blackhawks - NHL - Coach 3rd place finish.

Coach in 3 NHL All-Star Games

Received Milestone Award from NHL - coached 542 victories in NHL career.

Only one other player besides myself in the history of hockey to have played on:

Memorial Cup   (Junior Championship of Canada)
Allan Cup   (Senior Championship of Canada)
Stanley Cup   (N.H.L.)

and as you have seen in the above resume' I played and coached 2 Allan Cups and played on 2 Stanley Cups.

"Oh, what the hell," he roared.

He opened the door, a car hit it, tore it off the hinges and the door kept going right on down the street.

But it didn't faze Dad. He just got out and walked away, while Bobby and I stood there and gave the cabbie all the money we had to pay for the door.

I remember him coming to see me play the first time we played in Montreal. Everyone tells me I've made this story up, but it's the honest truth.

It's been a while now since this tradition was carried out, but when the Canadiens used to score a big goal, the fans would throw their toe-rubbers on the ice in appreciation. They were only a buck a piece and it's kind of like the squid in Detroit or the rats in Miami. The toe-rubbers would get thrown and then some employees would come out with scrapers and take the toe-rubbers off the ice.

We went in the back door and past all the ice-making equipment and as I was heading towards the dressing room, Dad grabs me and puts his arm around me, which was pretty unusual. I thought he was going to give me some important fatherly advice. "Listen son. When you're out there tonight and Béliveau scores, get me a size ten and a half."

FIVE

And Then There Were Two

*W*hen Bobby was 13, he went to Hespeler to start his career with the Junior Blackhawks. However, there was some hesitation on my mother's part to let him go because he was so young. My dad was familiar with the hockey world though, and having had the chance to go to a Toronto Maple Leafs camp, he thought Bobby should head off to give hockey a try. It was a big deal for him to see Bobby get a chance to perhaps play in the NHL and both Mom and Dad knew Bobby was a special talent. It was either put the light under the bushel or let it out.

Bob Wilson was the chief scout with the Blackhawks and he guaranteed that he'd put Bobby in a nice home and make sure he went to school. In our little town it was a pretty big deal. It was a company town, and nearly everyone followed Bobby. I was only eight in 1953 when he left for the Blackhawks farm team.

Bobby wasn't the only one in the family to have a chance to make it in hockey. My brothers Garry and Ron both had opportunities, as well. They were the best players on their respective teams. It's funny, though, because there really is a fine line between making it and not making it. It's usually whether you believe in yourself. They both wanted to make it as much as I did, but I don't think they ever believed they could really get to the NHL. Even when they were better than I was, I still thought I was going to make it while they never really decided that was what they wanted to do. They did lots of other things and they weren't as committed as I was.

My big chance came in 1960 when I was 15 and received an invitation to the Blackhawks Junior training camp in St. Catharines. It was the year they won the Memorial Cup and at the end of camp there was one spot being fought over between me and Murray Hall, who was 19. We waited outside the coach's door in the hotel to be called in and told the news. Murray went in and when he came out, he was excited because they were going to keep him. So I knew, by the time I went into meet with the coach, that I wasn't going to be there. But I was only 15 and it had been an amazing experience to be at training camp with future NHLers like Ray Cullen, Bill Speer, Doug Robinson, and Roger Crozier.

After I got cut, I went home to Pointe Anne, where the Blackhawks thought I was going to play for the Junior B team in Belleville. Red Gravelle was the coach of the Belleville team. He lived in Trenton, was a member of the Air Force and had played hockey at a high level. There were three Hulls on the team at the time, since both Ron and Garry played as well. Eventually only two of us would stay.

We used to play in Kingston, and Red would pick us up. A few games into the season, Red stopped by and Ron said, "Red, my brother Dennis needs his skates sharpened before the game."

"No, he doesn't," Red replied.

"What do you mean he doesn't need his skates sharpened?"

"He doesn't need his skates sharpened 'cause he's not playing!"

He was a nice guy who worked with me in practice, but said I should go and play Midget level rather than sit on the bench for another year. I dropped down a league, and by then, I could really shoot the puck, especially for someone my age. I'd regularly score seven or eight goals a game. "You should have had ten goals," Dad would say. "That was ridiculous."

Part way through the season, Bob Wilson, the chief scout for the Blackhawks, came down to Pointe Anne. It was exciting, at 15, to have the chief scout of the Blackhawks watching. He came to the house for dinner. We had a very big dinner, which was standard at the Hull household, and then Dad drove Wilson, Ron, Garry, and me to Belleville.

My brothers went to the dressing room and my dad and Bob were sitting around talking about how Bobby and the Blackhawks were doing.

Suddenly Wilson said, "Shouldn't you be going soon?"

"Going where?" I said.

"Well, going to get dressed."

"I don't play on this team," I replied.

This seemed to confuse him. After all, the Blackhawks had expected I would play for Belleville.

"You don't understand," he said. "The Blackhawks have sent me here to watch you play. There's got to be some mistake. I've got to see you play. I've got to make a report of your progress."

He seemed a little exasperated by the whole situation.

"Well, I don't play."

Gordie Bell, who had played part of a season as a goaltender with the Leafs in 1945–46, was the coach of the Junior team at the time, having replaced Gravelle part way through the season. Wilson went over to Bell and said, "I'm here to watch Dennis play."

Bell couldn't quite figure it out and seemed as confused as I was by the whole situation.

"He isn't on our team," Bell said.

But since the Blackhawks supported the team, Wilson asked if he could approach the other team, which was from Kingston, and see if they would allow me in the lineup. I was Midget age at the time, and Wilson didn't think the team would be too concerned if a 15-year-old played.

"Okay," Bell said. "I'll check. You're the guys who foot the bills."

He went over to the Kingston bench and asked if he could put a Midget player in the lineup. The opposing coach didn't have a problem with that. But when Bell came back and said everything was going ahead, it created another problem nobody anticipated. Now someone on the team had to get undressed. I felt like an idiot.

Bell walked into the dressing room and said, "The Blackhawks want to see Dennis play, so someone's going to have to get undressed."

"I will," someone said, though I couldn't tell who it was right away.

I looked and realized it was my brother Garry. He proceeded to take his equipment off. I wore his equipment, skates and all. I had a goal to tie the game and assisted on the winner in overtime. I may never have had a chance to go to St. Catharines if not for Garry's generosity.

I guess all went well, because the next fall I went to the St. Catharines Blackhawks' training camp, to try out for the TeePees. Garry came with me. It was different for my parents to send us to St. Catharines after Bobby had been there. They didn't see it as any big deal, and anyway, my old man thought it would be easier and cheaper to board Garry and me out than it would be to have to pay to feed us at home. He never even took us to St. Catharines. He just put us on a train.

When we arrived in St. Catharines, I realized that as committed as I was to being a hockey player, Garry was probably more committed to having a good time. He was a wild guy. We checked into the hotel in St. Catharines as roommates, and the first thing I noticed was there were two beds! I couldn't believe it. Our house in Pointe Anne was so small and there were so many Hulls that we'd never actually had a room of our own. It's clear this impressed me more than it impressed Garry.

Our room was right by the fire escape and soon after we got into the room, Garry disappeared and I didn't see him for two days. In fact, he never went on the ice. It was a chance of a lifetime, but it ended up taking the team officials two days to locate him.

I, on the other hand, made the team.

SIX

Connecting with Dunk Schram

*Y*ou had to be pretty tough to get through Junior hockey. It was certainly a lot more physical than the NHL turned out to be, and there were players who would fight with me because I was Bobby's brother and they could make a reputation out of it. It doesn't really make sense because there was little to be gained by fighting with me, but it only happened early in my career. The first two years, I had some problems because I was young and had a lot to learn, but I thought I knew it all. I also thought I could play with anyone, but I only scored six goals in the first year and didn't play much. The next year I scored six goals again though I played a bit more. It started to hit me that maybe I couldn't do it, that the NHL was too much and that maybe I wouldn't make it.

I lived with Fred Stanfield on Thomas Street in St. Catharines for most of the time I was in Junior, and part way through my third season, I talked to him about my concerns.

"You know, Freddy, I don't think I'm going to make it," I said.

"Ah, Dennis, you've just got to keep going," he said. "We're getting better all the time."

But I wasn't as convinced. I got ready to go home for Christmas and had pretty much decided I wasn't going to make it. But there was still a game left.

I knew what an NHL player did the day of the game because I'd been around Bobby. I always ate at 1 PM and slept in the afternoon. I did that religiously. I'd do anything to be like an NHL player.

But I'd made a big decision for a 16-year-old, and this day I didn't practise my regular routine. I had finally come to the conclusion that I wouldn't make it in hockey. When I went to play Niagara Falls that night, a big weight seemed to be lifted.

It's funny, because that was the best game I ever played to that point. I scored two goals, one on a breakaway. It seemed to happen all at once. That season I finished with 19 goals and the following year I scored 48. I was on my way.

*I*t was during my last couple of years with the St. Catharines TeePees that I became noted for my slapshot. There have been writers and spectators who have said it was even harder than Bobby's shot, but there were lots of times it didn't go exactly where I thought it was headed. In St. Catharines, between periods, the fans used to head out of the arena and across the street to the Queensway Hotel to have a beer because alcohol wasn't served at the games. Early in the second period of a game in the last year I was with the team I got the puck and took a big shot. Not all the spectators were back from the Queensway, so they didn't see the shot, which hit the crossbar, went over the screen, and out a window at the top of the stands.

Before the ref could drop another puck for the face-off, a man came running into the arena with one hand on his head and the puck in his other hand. Clearly, the shot which had gone out the window had struck this man on the head as he was coming back to the game after finishing his beer. A big cheer went throughout the arena and the guy waited for me after the game. His name was Dunk Schram and we remained friends for many years after that shot. The same year, I took a shot in Hamilton that hit the screen behind the net that protected the goal light. In this case, though, the shot went through the net and knocked the light off. For a while no one was certain what to do. In the end, the officials decided to go back to the early days of the game, when the goal judge would wave a hanky if anyone scored. So that one shot set hockey in Hamilton back forty years.

*I*n my last year in Junior, Bobby Orr was just starting with Oshawa as a 14-year-old. But I was 18 or 19, and much older and stronger. We were in the playoffs and were up by three games in the series and would head to Montreal to play the Junior Canadiens if we won. Though Orr played for Oshawa, his team's arena wasn't yet finished (it had earlier burned down) and the game was held in Bowmanville. It was close enough to Pointe Anne that my sister Maxine came down to watch me play.

During the game Orr slashed me a couple of times and though I'd heard he was supposed to be this phenomenon, I didn't know anything much about him. I wasn't going to let him get away with the slashes, so I gave him a swat near the end of the game. However, the damage, to me at least, was already done. I took a hit from Orr during my last shift of the game and tore the ligaments in my left knee. I was determined to keep playing though, so I got the leg taped up and was preparing to drive with our coach, Ken Campbell, to Montreal.

We went out to the car and this lady came up and smacked me with her purse. It was Bobby Orr's aunt.

"What do you think you're doing, picking on a 14-year-old?" she yelled.

All of a sudden my sister Maxine came over and grabbed her. It looked like a fight was going to break out, so I had to separate the two of them. That was my first encounter with Orr, but it certainly wouldn't be my last one.

We went on to Montreal to play the Junior Canadiens and the series went seven games. Throughout my whole career, I always ended up playing the finals against the Canadiens and almost always lost in seven games. It was so close. Due to the knee injury I'd sustained while playing Oshawa, I was put in a hospital in Montreal and the day of the game a doctor came and froze my knee so I could play that night. I went back in the hospital and the next day they froze my knee again. This went on for the entire seven games.

Fortunately nothing bad happened, although we lost in the seventh game.

Montreal always seemed to have a little extra.

Fred and I had lived together in St. Catharines, but during my last year with the TeePees the lady who owned the house decided not to have any hockey players stay with her any longer. Not that we were bad, it's just that she'd had players for a long time and wanted a break.

One of our teammates, John Brennemen, was living with Jimmy and Mary Ayre, a couple who boarded players, and Fred and I heard she was looking for a couple of hockey players to live at her house. We contacted her and went for an interview, after which Mary decided we could stay. She was a tremendous lady and a great cook. She even allowed us to have the other guys over for parties in her basement.

There was a girl who used to walk by the house on her way to and from school. She lived a few doors down and I saw her regularly because Fred had a car and we'd often drive by her on the way to practice.

While heading to the arena on one of these occasions I saw the girl walking and told Fred to stop and ask her if she wanted a ride. We stopped and she introduced herself as Sue Newman and hopped in the car. The year was 1964. We got married the following year after I had started playing in Chicago. I always introduce her as my first wife, especially given Bobby's tendencies and his three marriages.

SEVEN

The Man from Humboldt

Playing Junior was amazing, partly because the team was owned by the Blackhawks and we were treated and expected to act like NHL players, despite the fact we were only teenagers. Everyone on the team wanted to emulate the players in the National Hockey League, and because we wore the same uniform as the Blackhawks, it was clear to everyone that the next step was the NHL. At the time there were no players coming out of universities or American colleges.

Other kids at school also looked at us differently. Everyone thought it was a big deal that we were playing for the Blackhawks' team in St. Catharines. Girls used to always hang out with us, and we were invited to parties all the time. It was fabulous, everything I'd ever dreamed about as a kid growing up in a small town.

The summer before my first training camp, I received a note that would change my life, though. It was from the Blackhawks, saying that I'd been invited to the NHL training camp in St. Catharines. It was like a dream.

But I was also aware of the reality of the situation. There were 80 guys trying to make the team and I didn't think my chances were that good. I just kept watching guys get cut and wondered who would be next. It was on the ice in St. Catharines that I finally found out I had made the team.

Billy Wirtz Jr., the owner of the team, came to the arena one day towards the end of camp and talked to Billy Reay, the coach of the Blackhawks.

Soon afterwards Billy came up to me while I was on the ice.

"Can you find your way to Chicago?" he asked.

"I've walked from Point Anne to Belleville," I said. "I'm prepared to walk to Chicago."

I was 19 and heading to the NHL. It was also exciting because Fred had been told he'd made the team as well, so the two of us were going to Chicago together. (At the time, I thought Fred and I would play our whole careers together. But in 1967 he was traded in the worst exchange in the history of hockey, with the Blackhawks moving Ken Hodge, Phil Esposito, and Fred to Boston in exchange for Jack Norris, Gilles Marotte and my future linemate, Pit Martin.)

It seemed like a big step, but I'd played against a lot of guys who were in the NHL, like Rod Gilbert and Jean Ratelle, who had both played for the Guelph Junior team. Gilbert and Ratelle used to get called up to New York frequently. Oftentimes, we'd play against them on a Saturday and they'd play for the New York Rangers on Sunday. It was a good way to gauge yourself and determine whether a player was good enough for the NHL. All the teams used to shuttle Junior players back and forth, and guys would occasionally play as many as seven or eight games in the NHL in one year while still remaining Junior players (i.e., amateurs). I'd played against them and done well, so I thought I was ready.

It was during this training camp that I became acquainted with Glenn Hall, one of the best goalies to ever play the game. He was like a cat, even though, when I started in 1964–65, he was nearing the end of his career with the Blackhawks. He always painted his barn every fall towards the end because he hated going to training camp and that way he had an excuse for not showing up on time.

He was a great guy, but he had this funny lisp. Just a little lisp though, which made "s" sound like "th" when he spoke. And it was just the thing a 19-year-old would choose to pick on. Besides Fred Stanfield, Doug Jarrett was the third in the group of friends who came to training camp together. There used to be a sign near the training camp that said "Toronto — 66 miles." We were such smartasses that we'd get on the bus, sitting near the back, and either Doug or I would say, "Wonder how far it is to Toronto?"

"Thikthty-thikth miles," Glenn would always reply.

We did it three or four times and then he caught on.

"How many miles is it to Toronto?" I asked.

"A hundred and thirty-two return, you thmartaleck cock-thuckerth!"

When the season started, I ended up sitting in the dressing room next to him before the start of my first game. I knew he was a great goalie but had no idea that he got sick to his stomach before every game. But since I was one of the rookies who had made fun of him, I was fair game and he wouldn't leave me alone.

Before the game he got up and was sick. Throughout the dressing room, you could hear him vomiting in the washroom.

When he came back, I asked whether he got sick before every game.

"Only thinth you've joined the team," came the reply.

Now I realized I was going to get a hard time from Glenn forever. It was all in fun, but he wouldn't let up. A few games into my first season, we were playing in old Madison Square Garden and when Glenn lost his shutout, with a minute to go and up 6–1, Billy Reay sent me out.

The face-off was in the New York end. As we were lining up, Glenn began banging his stick on the ice and the referee, Art Skov, skated down the ice to see what was going on.

Art came back and came over to me and said, "You're Dennis Hull, right? Well, Glenn wants to see you."

I skated all the way down the ice and the New York fans were going nuts, screaming and carrying on. I was concerned that I'd done something wrong and Glenn was angry. But I'd just got on the ice and couldn't figure out what I could possibly have done in such a short period of time.

"Glenn, what's up?"

"Lithen kid, don't thcrew thith game up," was all he said to me before ushering me back to the other end of the ice. I'd been had.

The funny thing about Glenn is that he didn't actually like being a hockey player. He hated playing and the only thing he hated more than playing was practising.

There were only two things that really stopped Glenn from not playing. One factor was, during the first year I played, the team carried only one goalie.

And because the team didn't carry a second goalie, it was often the trainer who would play if the starter got hurt. The second year I was at training camp, one of the goalies was a guy named Art Lariviere. The procedure at the end of training camp was always the same: part way through camp the players stand outside general manager Tommy Ivan's door and he'd bring you in and sign you or send you somewhere.

This time, I was behind Art when he went into meet Ivan.

When he came out, he had a quizzical look on his face.

"What are you doing, Art?"

"Well, I'm going to Chicago."

I was confused. Art was a good guy, but about the tenth best goalie at camp.

"Really, you're going to Chicago?"

"Yeah, but that's the good news," he said. "The other part is that I'm going as the trainer."

He never actually played, and after my first year, we had two goalies.

In fact, I remember a time when Dave Dryden got called out of the seats at Maple Leaf Gardens and was asked to play. The goalie got hurt and the PA announced, "Is Dave Dryden in the audience?", which is kind of like asking, "Is there a doctor in the house?"

Even though Glenn hated playing, he couldn't quit because he was so good. Practices were always a good opportunity to get back at him for playing jokes on me and I took full advantage.

When we'd take shooting drills, Glenn always hated facing Bobby and me. He'd get as far from the centre of the net as he could, hoping Bobby and I would shoot at the net. But we'd shoot the puck and hit him anyway. And then he'd get out of his net, leaving his stick behind and we'd shoot it at him again.

Then he'd skate into the corner and we'd still pick him out and shoot it at him. He'd get so angry that he'd turn red.

"Billy, the Hull boyth are thooting at me again!"

It's funny though, because he eventually found out where we got our shot from. In 1966, we were playing in Toronto and my dad, who was 55 at the time, came out to skate with us.
Glenn was in the net and goaded Dad into letting a shot go.

"Come on Mithter Hull, take a thot," he said.

My dad, as I've said, was a pretty good player in his time. He skated in and rifled one off the crossbar.

"Why you old thon of a bitch," Glenn said. "No wonder your boyth are the way they are." He also liked to give Bobby and me a hard time about not playing defence. After a game, when he saw us having a shower, he always said, "Aw, there'th the Hull boyth. Haven't theen you thinth warmup."

In 1966–67 I had 20 goals with six games left in the season and Glenn approached me.

"You think you're thuch a big thot," he said. "Weally big thot. Big goal thcorer. Big hot thot, eh? Bet you don't thcore 25 goalth in the theathon. I'll put 50 buckth on it."

He was a big star, so I didn't think I should turn him down.

The next night in Boston I got a goal, I scored two in the following game in Detroit and got one in Montreal. The last goal I scored was in New York. It was the 264th goal scored by

Chicago that year, the most any team had scored in a single season, and my 24th.

Glenn didn't play because we were already in first place and, with the score 3–2, New York pulled their goalie. I managed to get the puck and made a break.

Jim Neilson was trying to cut me off, and all the while Glenn was on the bench yelling to him. "Get that bathtard!" he screamed as Neilson skated down towards me. I scored goal number 25 on the empty net, but Hall never paid up. I still remind him.

Despite all of that, we did have a great rapport. His record of playing goal in 502 consecutive games will probably never be broken. One time during the first period of a game during that streak, Jimmy Pappin, who was playing for Toronto, hit Glenn in the face with a shot. Glenn took 25 stitches in the mouth, but came back in the third period to continue playing. He "retired" in 1967, but on being drafted by St. Louis, continued to play until 1971. He simply hated being an adult yet being told he couldn't go out for a beer. He didn't even come to training camp in 1966 because he said he was quitting.

The team officials finally talked him into coming back about 15 games into the season and well into November. The circus was in the stadium in Chicago at the time Glenn was supposed to come back to the team, so we were practising at an outdoor rink which had no walls, only a roof. I remember it being terribly cold and after practising for 10 minutes, Glenn stormed off the ice.

"I didn't come back to play in thith goddamn cold," he said. "No way."

And with that he was off the ice, having taken only five or six shots.

We went to New York the following night and he shut out the Rangers. Despite his abilities, if you met Glenn, you'd never know he was a star. I remember coming back from a practice and he got pulled over by a cop. Glenn pulled out his licence and handed it to the officer.

"Oh, you're Glenn Hall," the officer said. "I'm not going to give you a ticket."

"You goddamn well *are* going to give me a ticket," he said, making the officer write one out. It was just another sign of how much he hated anyone treating him differently.

A couple of years ago they had a special day for him in his home town of Humboldt, Saskatchewan. The town had built a new arena and part of the arena was going to contain a hall of fame for local athletes. Of course they were electing Glenn to it and he invited me down to speak at the dinner.

He went to introduce me, with his mother sitting right next to me. I think she must have been 85. I was really anticipating the introduction, and finally Glenn got up and went to the podium. I thought he was going to give me a big welcome. He walked up to the microphone and looked at his mother and then motioned towards me.

"Don't believe a goddamn word he thayth."

EIGHT

Shadowing Mr. Hockey

*I*n my first year I played quite a few games and scored 10 goals. I thought I'd done pretty well — if I'd scored 10 goals as a rookie today, I'd probably be signed to a million-dollar contract. The problem I faced in Chicago came not from other players, but from the fans. Writers had talked about me and the fans heard there was another Hull coming who would be just like Bobby. But Chicago fans didn't know the game like, for example, the Canadian fans. They were disappointed that I wasn't Bobby. Of course, I was disappointed by that too.

But when it turned out I wasn't going to be a replica of Bobby, they took it out on me, which was unnerving. In 1964, I had been voted the most popular player on the St. Catharines team. After only a few months in Chicago, I was the least popular. But I hadn't changed. I was still the same player.

However, when I played in Toronto or Montreal, the fans liked the way I played. The disdain of the fans in Chicago was tough on me, because I was only 19. But Billy really helped me through it and explained that the fans didn't know that much about hockey and that my teammates understood I could play. That was fine, but the problem affected my play. I scored 303 goals in my career, but more than 200 came when I was on the road. If you look at it one way, I might have been a 400-goal scorer if I'd played only on the road. It should be the other way around: most players score more on their home ice. In 1970–71 I scored 40 goals and the fans still booed me. There was no way to win them over. Bobby scored 44 goals that year and he was treated as a hero. It bothered me, but it made me look forward to going on the road to play.

The other problem I had was my attitude, which Billy straightened out quickly. The first game I played was at home against Boston and I sat on the bench until the end of the game. Billy had told me he wanted to start me off slowly, but I'd just come from St. Catharines where I'd scored 48 goals. I thought I was ready to play every day in the NHL.

With 12 seconds to go in the game and the score 3–0 in our favour, Billy finally told me to get on the ice.

"With 12 seconds left?" I asked.

"Sit down and be in my office right after the game," he said curtly. I knew I'd done something wrong, but was young and thought I was really hot stuff. I thought I *deserved* to play.

I went in the office after the game and was there for an hour. I couldn't hear when I came out because Billy had spent the whole time yelling at me. However, his method was effective; after that, I never questioned him about a coaching move again.

The next game I played in was in Detroit. Though I'd made it to the NHL, I wasn't certain I was going to be sticking around. There were simply so many good players that you never knew how long it would be before someone better would come along. The day of the game we went out to practise at 11 in the morning. We finished our skate and loosened up and though we were always told the morning warmup was just to check out our stick and skates and other equipment, I think its purpose was to keep guys from staying in bed all day.

As things were winding up, Billy called everyone over to the goal at one end to give the team some final instructions before the game that night.

"OK, we're having dinner at London Chop House and the bus leaves at five," he said, before continuing to explain our schedule for the day.

As Billy began telling us what we were going to do, stragglers were taking their time getting back and were trying to shoot pucks over the glass at the other end of the rink. At the opposite end of the ice were two off-duty policemen who would always come and watch the practices at the Olympia.

After a few minutes of this, Billy was getting edgy and decided to put an end to the shooting.

"Aw, come on. There's only one guy who can shoot the puck over the glass from one end of the ice to the other and he plays on the other team," he said referring to Gordie Howe. Just as he said that, I took a puck and fired it. It went over the glass at the other end and hit the seat between the two cops. Everyone turned and looked at Billy Reay.

"Okay, now there are two guys."

Howe had always been an idol to all the Hulls as we grew up. I just loved the way he played and the way he was with people away from the arena. Once a year my dad used to take us to a game at Maple Leaf Gardens, even before Bobby was playing. My brother Garry and I often used to go together. The gates would open and you could buy a rush seat for two dollars. We'd always be there early. My dad liked to stand next to the end blues, so Garry and I would run up the stairs and spread out so there would be room for our dad when he came. He'd saunter up and we'd separate and he'd stand in the middle.

I remember seeing Gordie play at one of those games and thinking he was fantastic because he wasn't flashy, but he did everything so well.

On another one of our pilgrimages to the Gardens, Bobby tried to get Gordie's autograph after a game the Red Wings had lost. Bobby, who was 12 at the time, waited out by the team bus with scores of other kids. Gordie came out of the Gardens and as Bobby asked him for an autograph, Howe just walked right by him. Bobby couldn't understand how his hero could do this to him.

Bobby walked back towards Dad and was pretty upset.

"Well, they lost so don't feel bad," Dad said as sympathetically as he could. While he was telling Bobby this, Gordie came off the bus, found Bobby and signed an autograph for him. I don't know why Gordie came back, but Bobby always remembered the incident.

Perhaps it's fitting that during this game in Detroit, Billy eventually sent me out to shadow Howe. For most of the game, I simply sat on the bench and enjoyed watching my idol. I was so close to Gordie that I could stick my glove over the boards and touch him when he skated by. It was sort of mind-boggling for a 19-year-old. When Glenn lost his shutout and it was 8–1, I finally got the call to go out on the ice. There were only a couple of minutes left in the game, but I now knew better than to argue with Billy.

"Get out there and watch Howe," Reay said to me.

It wasn't really necessary — I was pretty sure I could see him well enough from the bench.

But Billy insisted I get on the ice, so I went out and stood next to Howe, who wasn't skating around, but standing in one place, blinking regularly, like he always did. I knew there wasn't anything I could say: Howe never talked to the opposition.

On my line were Billy Hay at centre and Eric Nesterenko on right wing. Hay won the draw and passed it to Nesterenko. I was heading towards centre ice and I remember thinking that if I got the puck I might even get a shot on net. I could even get a goal! These thoughts were passing through my head when, all of a sudden, my skates were no longer on the ice.

It was Howe — he'd grabbed me by the back of the pants with one hand and picked me up off the ice and said, "Where do you think you're going?"

"Wherever you are going . . . sir," I said.

Despite this, Billy used to always send me out to watch Gordie.

In 1968, Denis DeJordy was our goalie the year we ended up in last place. DeJordy was a great minor league goaltender, but had struggled in the NHL. Because of Denis' poor playing, Billy wanted me to keep Howe from shooting when he got over the blue line.

"Watch Howe, and try to get him to shoot it from inside the red line," Billy said, explaining the approach to use on Howe. "Make him come to centre and make him shoot it. Don't let him go wide."

I did exactly as Billy said. Howe got the puck and went down the right side. I had just forced him to centre ice, when he let go with one of his wrist shots. It flew by me, right into the top right corner of the net.

I went back to the bench and Billy was waiting for me.

"I told you to watch him," he said, acting as if he were angry with me, before breaking into laughter.

A lot of people don't understand that the players also have favourites, and Gordie was mine. People are always throwing around the term "star" or "superstar." When a good player gets a puck, people anticipate it and sit on the edge of their seats. I remember Bobby getting the puck and getting ready to shoot and people in the seats would stand up. But you know you're watching a superstar when the players on the opposing team are standing up. That's how you tell if the player deserves the term.

The connection between me and Gordie has been there for a while. In fact, Howe used to write hockey tips, and I was actually in one of them. It remains one of the biggest thrills of my career. In his column, Howe was talking about keeping with a player from one end of the ice to the other, until you were sure the player wasn't going to get a chance on net. Howe said he was playing against me and, on this occasion, I was carrying the puck all the way down the ice. He covered me all the way, and then, as we got within a couple of feet of the goal line, he turned and went to the point, which was also his job when the puck was in our end.

Except this time Howe didn't follow me all the way and I fired the puck right over the shoulder of the goalie. The point was to stay with your man all the way, and I thought it was amazing to use me as the example.

⬤

I played my first all-star game in 1969 in Montreal. The Blackhawks had played in Montreal on the Saturday night before the all-star game, which was being played on a Monday, so I decided to stay instead of travelling back and forth between Montreal and Chicago. My team's dressing room for the game was the home dressing room, so the Chicago trainer packed my bag and took it over.

I followed it over soon afterwards because I had a special request to make and I thought if I got there early, maybe it would happen.

I ran into the trainer, who was from Quebec, and said, "Can I dress next to Gordie Howe?"

"It's a funny ting, you know," he said. "Because Gordie Howe just called from Detroit and asked to dress next to you."

It was hard to believe: Howe knew that I was such a fan that he'd called and said, "Put Dennis Hull next to me." I was amazed.

And I'm not among his critics who think he played too long. He told me that the last year he played in Hartford, he was among the top scorers on the team and he was 52. The management called him in after the season was over and said they thought he should retire.

His reply very much sums up the man.

"Why, do you think I'm going to lose it over the summer?"

I still run into Gordie every so often. A few years ago we were playing a charity golf match in Halifax. We had to play early in the day, because Gordie had to fly out in the afternoon. The round started at 6:30 AM and, without a warmup, Howe shot a 72.

When we finished, I said, "Gordie, it's not fair. You're the greatest hockey player and a fabulous golfer. It's just not fair."

"Well, Dennis," he said, "you should see me bowl."

It was during my rookie year that I met my first hippie, in attitude at least. His name was Eric Nesterenko, and he was also my linemate. Billy always thought linemates should room together because they'd become friends and work better on the ice as a result. In fact, being friends with your roommate always paid off around curfews. Billy rarely checked curfews because if he told us to be in at 11 PM, then we were generally in around that time. But if Billy saw you after curfew and you weren't with your linemate, you were in big trouble.

The thing was that Eric wasn't quite normal, something I noticed when we roomed together on my first road trip. We were sitting in the room watching TV when a commercial came on. Nesterenko shut the TV off and sat staring at his watch. After one minute, he'd turn the TV back on. It turned out he hated commercials, but I was only 19 and thought this was kind of strange. I came to the conclusion that Nesterenko, who was 30 at the time, was just old and weird, with an emphasis on old.

The next day I approached Billy.

"Can I have a younger roommate?"

The answer was no, which allowed me to see some of Eric's other peculiarities. During my rookie year, the team went on a road trip once which was 12 days long. Our per diem was only $10 so we had $120 for the trip. We went to New York and Eric went down to the Village. The next day he came to breakfast and approached me.

"Dennis, could you lend me a couple of bucks?"

I don't know how he normally got by, but this time all his allowance was gone.

He also would smoke strange things, but of course it was the sixties. He was very intellectual and cerebral, a bit strange, nearly 6-foot-4, and very thin.

He went to the Village one time and he thought he might have smoked something funny. When he got back to the hotel, he told me the story of his evening.

"I met this girl tonight and she invited me back to her apartment on 2nd Avenue. When we got there, she told me she was going into her room to put on something a little more comfortable. When she got back, all she was wearing was this negligée and she sat down on the sofa next to me. She was a short, chubby girl, but I made a move on her anyway and she jumped out of the way. I tried it again and she jumped out of the way, but faster. Pretty soon I was chasing her all around the room but I couldn't catch her. So I left.

"Tonight after the game, I'm going back there to see if I was just hallucinating."

The next day he told me he went back after the game and stood on the street corner where he could see into the girl's apartment through a window. There he saw a short fat man chasing the girl all over the room. Eric says he started to laugh. Eventually a policeman came by.

"What's so funny?" the cop asked.

"Well, look up there," Eric said, pointing at the window.

"If you think that's funny, you should have seen the tall skinny guy chasing her last night."

Up, Down, and Back Again

I went to the Stanley Cup against the Canadiens in my first
season with the Blackhawks, though I didn't play much once
we got there. The series that we lost went to seven games, and it
was the first of three times I'd lose the Stanley Cup to Montreal.

Perhaps because I didn't play much, I still don't find much
about the series very memorable.

However, I did get to play a shift against Jean Béliveau.
Béliveau, who went on to win the Conn Smythe Trophy, was
playing some of his best games. During that series, Esposito
was playing with Chico Maki and Bobby and there was a face-off
to the right of Glenn. Billy called Esposito to the boards and
leaned over me towards Phil.

"After you lose the draw to Béliveau, stay with him."

Phil thought Billy might have lacked a little confidence in him.

Even after I started playing, Béliveau was a hero of mine and
still remained my dad's idol. In fact, Dad thought everything
would be fine in Canada if they'd only make Béliveau the king
of the country.

Billy thought in order to take the series as seriously as possible,
we shouldn't talk to the other team, which we didn't, for the most
part. During the game, Béliveau was coming down on Pierre

Pilote. Pilote fell coming over the blue line, so I had to come off my wing and across the ice to deal with Béliveau. All I could do was slash him across the arms. He took the puck and flipped it into the corner.

He looked at me for a moment and said, "I did not expect that from you."

"Well, I'm sorry Jean," I said, and continued to apologize over and over. In fact I followed him all the way to the Canadiens' bench, telling him how sorry I was.

When I got back to our bench, Billy was angry.

"Don't be talking to the other players," he said.

"But, Billy, I wasn't talking to him — I was apologizing to him."

It was during my first season that Billy Reay started to become the most influential figure in my life. Without a doubt he taught me more about life than my dad ever did. Despite his impact, I still struggled in my second season. I had such a tough time that I was sent down to the Blackhawks minor league team in St. Louis. It was the sophomore jinx. I'd read about players having a difficult time in their second season and then I found out exactly what it was.

The first year you work so hard to get to the NHL and it's so exciting. And though it wasn't a conscious thing, I must have let up a bit in my second year. Just when I thought I had it made, it all came tumbling down. In the NHL you can never think you've got it made. It doesn't work that way.

I was in St. Louis for 40 games and I hated every minute of it. I played all the time, but I thought I was forgotten by the Blackhawks. It was during that time that Pierre Pilote, the Blackhawks captain, showed up to watch me play. Pierre had been injured, so he came down and stayed with me in St. Louis for a couple of days. It was a big lift and an amazing gesture on his part.

Pilote was undoubtedly one of the best captains the Black-hawks ever had. He was a great liaison between management and the owners, and he'd come and tell us about rumours and trades. On top of all of this, he was a great player, which is a must if you want to be a true captain of a team.

He often played when Bobby was on the ice, which worked out well for Bobby. He was a great playmaker, except the guys on the right wing would always complain. He would skate up the middle and turn and fake to the guy on the right wing. Then he'd turn and pass it to Bobby.

"How come you never give it to me?" right winger Ken Wharram used to ask.

"Well, you get 50 goals and I'll give it to you," was always Pierre's reply. Sometimes Bobby would go end-to-end and score.

Before the refs started strictly enforcing the rules, you could get away with a lot when it came to assists. In my first couple of seasons, after a goal was scored, the referee gave out the assists. Often the ref knew who scored the goal but wasn't certain who had the assist, which meant he had to ask the players on the ice.

"Me and some other guy," Pierre always said.

He was also very tough, especially for a man who wasn't that big. He had lots of penalty minutes and he'd still win the Norris Trophy. The penalty minutes came because of his use of his stick. His nickname was "the surgeon." And after he'd slashed or speared a guy, he always had this innocent look.

"I didn't do anything," he'd say.

But he never took any backwards steps, no matter how big his opponents were. I didn't like to fight, which became a problem when I got sent to St. Louis. Players on farm teams seemed to think they could make a name for themselves if they took a run at me. Fights in hockey in the fifties and sixties were different than they are now. Before expansion, each of us played against the other teams 14 times. After a while fights started because of frustration or general dislike. But you wouldn't see someone go out to start a fight.

When expansion came in 1967, the players on those teams couldn't compete with the Original Six because expansion didn't bring the new teams many stars. In order to compete, they tried to bring the stars down to their level through intimidation and premeditated fights. The aggressor would try to start something with a star player. Now I see it's changed again. The enforcers fight one another. The star is too valuable. But if you were in the NHL before expansion, you had to prove that you were tough enough to stay there. Once you proved you weren't going to back down, they left you alone. If you did back down, you could be driven right out of the league.

Fortunately for me, Doug Jarrett was in St. Louis at the time too, and he could handle himself better than I could. If anyone got on my case too much, he'd step in. Doug didn't get a lot of penalties, but people knew not to screw around with him. He'd been sent down around the same time I had and quickly became a lifelong friend. By 1966, we were both in Chicago to stay. Despite the fact Doug and I were great friends, he never got along with Billy. They fought like cats and dogs. For the most part, Billy was on him because he thought Doug could be better. I understood what Billy was doing, but a lot of times Doug took offence to it.

The one thing that really bugged Billy was that Doug was always late. Practice was at 10 AM, and Billy used to close the door to the rink right on the hour. Doug would always just make it as Billy was closing the door. But Doug had these wonderful excuses. It finally got to the point where Billy would call everyone to centre ice just to hear the excuses.

"Okay Dougie," Billy said, "what is it today?"

"Well, the dog ate my keys."

Billy looked perplexed.

"Both sets?"

On another occasion Doug said, "I got behind a school bus and I couldn't pass." Another time he said there was a train stuck on a crossing and he couldn't get by.

Perhaps the best excuse occurred on a day when he arrived just in time to make it on the ice. Everyone was waiting at centre ice because we knew Doug would be late and we'd get to hear one of his stories. He came skating onto the ice full blast, stopped in a shower of ice, and shouted, "Billy, don't pay the ransom, I got away!"

It's really just a case that Billy and Doug ended up together at the most inopportune times. We played in L.A. in February of 1968 and it was amazingly different from anywhere else we'd played. It was hot, the weather was wonderful, and there were palm trees everywhere.

The only problem was the Forum was hot as hell.

After the first period everyone was complaining that it was so hot on the ice. Between the first and second period, Billy had enough.

"I know it's hot out there, but it's the same for the other team. The next guy who says anything about how hot it is will get a $500 fine."

Doug started the first shift of the second period, finished, came to the bench and sat down next to me.

"Man, is it hot out there."

Billy came scrambling all the way down the bench. Just then Doug saw him.

"But it's just the way I like it," he added.

Dougie just couldn't stay out of Billy's way. We were at the Mount Royal Hotel in Montreal during my second year and we went out for drinks. We were a bit late in coming back in, and though Billy didn't check curfew regularly, Doug still had a plan in case he was around.

"Listen, we'll go up the stairway to the mezzanine," Dougie said. "That way we'll avoid the lobby."

I was following him, but what we forgot to figure into the equation was that Billy had been a player too. He was standing on the landing as we went up the stairs.

"Doug, we're in big trouble here," I said.

"Don't worry about it, just follow me."

We approached Billy, and Doug didn't flinch.

"Billy, I guess you couldn't sleep, either."

Regardless of the fact he was always late for everything, Doug became captain of the Blackhawks for one game against Pittsburgh. He was normally an assistant captain, but Stan Mikita was out with an injury and Pit was just coming back after having his appendix out. That made Doug captain.

Jimmy, Pit, and I started the game. As soon as the shift was over, there was a conference at the penalty box. It must have gone on for five minutes, which seems like forever when you're sitting on the bench. The word eventually came down that Billy had forgotten to put someone in the lineup.

Doug came over to the bench.

"Doug, come on," I said, aggravated at the situation. "Whoever isn't in the lineup, get him out and let's get going."

"It's you, Dennis."

I went skating out and headed towards the dressing room after only playing one shift, when a guy in the seats started talking to me.

"Hey, what's going on?" he said.

"Well, they forgot to put me in the lineup."

"But I came all the way from Nova Scotia just to see you play."

"I hope you watched carefully then," I answered.

*W*hat used to drive Billy crazy was the fact Doug would get it on the ankle with a shot in just about every game. Most guys could take it, but Doug would just crumple, throw his stick and gloves and fall into the ice, rolling around. There was so much equipment around that it looked like a lawn sale.

Billy tried to get Doug to wear ankle guards, but he didn't like them. Once, when we were playing in Montreal, Yvan Cournoyer was coming down the ice for the Canadiens, and everyone stood up on the bench to watch him make his move towards the net. Because we were all standing up, Billy didn't see Cournoyer's shot. But rather than hitting Doug on the ankle, like every other shot seemed to do, it went up his stick and hit him right in the forehead, knocking him out. He was out cold on the ice.

"What happened?" Billy asked. "Did Jarrett get hit in the ankle again?"

"No Billy, he got hit in the head," I replied.

"Oh, good," he said.

Despite his fragile ankles, Doug was also one of the best checkers in the NHL. He could skate backwards like the wind and would line a guy up and jump in his face and smash him with a hip check. We called him "Chairman of the boards." One time he lined Ron Ellis of the Leafs up and hit him so hard I thought he'd killed him.

Another time he had Mike Walton of the Leafs lined up and jumped in front of him. Walton saw him with just enough time to hit the ice. He slid on the ice and Doug went over top. I saw Walton after the game.

"God, I'm glad I saw him," Walton said. "If he'd have hit me, I'd be dead right now. Glad I put the downscope on."

In the mid-seventies, during the middle of his career, Doug began to fade late in games. He just didn't have any energy, and eventually was diagnosed with a deficiency that meant he had to eat very regularly. We were going into New York and we were sitting in the back row of a 727. The stewardesses served everyone but Doug. It was close to the time the plane was going to land and they wouldn't give Doug his dinner.

"But I want my dinner," he said.

"There's no time, sir," said the stewardess, "the plane is about to land."

"Get me my dinner!"

"But you only have 30 seconds."

"GET ME MY DINNER!"

She brought it out to him and he put the whole dinner, dessert and everything, into his mouth at once. Food was coming out the sides of his mouth. He was so busy stuffing it into his face that he pointed towards his bun, pointed at me and gestured for me to stuff the bun into his mouth, which I did. Finished, he slammed the table up and snapped it into place on the seat ahead of him and handed her the tray.

"Finished," he mumbled.

As the first year of expansion wore on, we found we had another problem. Some guys didn't like to fly, and now our flights were more regular and much longer. Doug was among the frequent fliers who were also frequently nervous about air travel. On one occasion we met Jimmy "The Greek" on a flight and Doug approached him.

"What's the odds of a bomb being on a plane?" Doug asked him.

"A million to one."

"Well then, what's the chance of two bombs being on a plane?"

"Obviously two million to one."

"Okay, I like those odds," Doug said. "I guess I'll have to carry a bomb onto every plane then."

We would always take on the same flight from Chicago to Boston and we got to know the pilot, Captain Frank. Eventually, he'd come back and visit us, which made Doug a bit nervous. He asked Doug why he always sat in the back row. After all, he said, it was the least comfortable part of the plane.

"Well, have you ever heard of one of these things *backing* into a mountain?" Doug asked.

Another time we were going to L.A. on the first 747 flight between Chicago and California. Because it was the inaugural flight, the staff of the plane were making a big party out of it. One of the stewardesses noticed us and decided we should run a contest. The winners would each get a magnum of champagne. It was during the sixties, when moustaches were in vogue, so Doug thought we should have a moustache contest.

He started walking up and down the aisles of the 747 and I followed him, writing his comments on a piece of paper.

As we walked down the aisles, all the men were combing their moustaches and trying to look as impressive as possible. When we were done looking at the moustaches, Doug retreated to his seat to look at the notes. Finally, after an hour and a half, Doug announced the winners: Two Italian ladies from New Jersey who hardly spoke English and had no idea why they'd won.

*I*n 1972 we went to play our farm team that was training in Las Vegas before travelling to Brantford to play the Penguins. Doug didn't want to leave because he was good at the tables. In fact, he won at craps and made Billy $700 which led Billy, uncharacteristically, to tell him what a great person he was.

On board the plane, Doug got this idea to show general manager Tommy Ivan and Billy that he didn't want to leave Las Vegas. At the time, Air Canada handed out Lifesavers and Doug took 16 packages and put them all in his mouth. He then handed me one and motioned to me that we should walk up to first class.

Tommy and Billy were there and Doug held his arm up in the air. At that point I stuck the remaining lifesaver up his nose and pulled his arm. He proceeded to spit 16 packages of lifesavers into a cup.

Billy wasn't impressed. We went back to sit down and a stewardess, carrying two pills, approached us.

"Are you Hull and Jarrett?"

"Yeah," I said.

"Well, these are from your coach."

"What are they?" Doug asked.

"They're smarten-up pills."

Finally, one day when we were practising prior to playing Montreal, Billy had enough.

"Doug, let's get this straight. I'm the coach and you're the player. Whatever I say you're going to do," Reay said.

"Okay then, Billy," Doug replied.

We went to Montreal and it was the day our players changed their numbers. The defencemen used to wear numbers in the twenties and Doug wore #20. Billy thought this was silly and changed the numbers. Doug went from #20 to #4. Cliff Korroll, who shot right-handed, began wearing #20. Someone got hurt in the game and both trainers had to help, leaving Billy alone on the bench. It was then that Doug broke his stick.

Instinctively Billy turned around and grabbed the stick with #20 written on it and handed it to Doug. Except it was Korroll's stick and Doug shot left-handed. But Doug was very aware that he'd told Billy he would do whatever the coach said.

So here was Doug in the middle of the Forum, playing right-handed. He didn't want to make Billy mad so he tried to slap it into the Canadiens' end. He looked terribly awkward. Billy came up to me on the bench.

"My, isn't Dougie shooting wonderfully right-handed tonight," he said.

TEN

"When You're as Drunk as We Are . . ."

I got called up at the end of the year in 1966 and played a bit in the playoffs. The next year I started in training camp. Billy was still a big supporter and said he thought I could play in the NHL, but that I needed more confidence.

On the first day of training camp Billy approached me. "I want you to relax and play the way you can play," he said, "because you're going to be here all year."

It was like a piano coming off my back. It was a great feeling. But early in the season it looked like I was going to be sent to St. Louis again and someone mentioned it to Bobby. At the time, if you played in more than six games, the team had to keep you. The seventh game came and Bobby told me although they were going to send me to the minors, they were still planning to dress me for the seventh game, but I would just sit on the bench.

"Here's what we're going to do," Bobby said. "When I start the game tonight and they drop the puck, I'm going to circle down around the defencemen and then I'll come to the bench. Nobody will be expecting me. Then you jump on."

It happened exactly that way, and as I was jumping on the ice,

Billy Reay grabbed me by the back of the sweater. But my skates had already hit the ice, and I'd officially registered my seventh game and so they had to keep me. I scored 25 goals that season and was in Chicago for good. The 1966–67 season was also the year we broke the "Curse of Muldoon." Pete Muldoon had been a former coach who was fired and then told the Blackhawks' management that because they let him go, the team would never end up in first place. The Curse lasted for over 30 years before we topped the league and put the myth to rest.

In 1967 hockey underwent its biggest change ever when the NHL expanded by six teams. It was a time filled with turmoil, but the social climate wasn't the only thing that caused problems. Expansion had its own set of strange occurrences, as well. For one thing, most players had never been to the West Coast, which confused some of them. Even a few years after expansion, players continued to be amazed by the new places they visited. In 1972, for example, a bunch of players rented a car when we were in San Francisco in order to take in the sites. J.P. Bordeleau was in the car and as we were driving along, J.P. noticed the island out in San Francisco Bay.

"Hey, Dennis, what's that?" J.P. said, pointing at Alcatraz.

"Hawaii," I said.

"Really?" he questioned. "I didn't know you could see it from the shore." These weren't intellectual giants I played with. They weren't splitting atoms in their spare time.

On another occasion something similar happened with Alain Daigle, who played with the Blackhawks in the mid-seventies. He had been a great Junior player and was one of the first French-Canadians the Blackhawks had drafted after he scored 90 goals the year before in Junior. But on the first day of training camp, I realized he couldn't speak a word of English. He also couldn't skate very well.

After the first day, I was skating around and Billy Reay came up.

"Can you imagine," he said, "we've drafted the only French Canadian in history who can't skate."

In February of Alain's first season, we went to Vancouver. Everybody was on the bus except Alain. The team had given us visas that allowed us to go back and forth across the border. You had to carry your visa whenever you travelled outside the country with the team. We sat on the bus for 40 minutes and finally Alain got on. You could tell Billy was angry because he was really turning red.

"OK Alain, what happened?" Reay asked.

"I forget my visa," the Frenchman replied.

"You forgot your visa? Didn't you know we are going to Vancouver?"

"Yeah," he replied, "but I did not know it was in Canada."

*I*t was in 1967 that Tommy Ivan made the worst trade in NHL history, when he dumped Phil Esposito, Ken Hodge, and Fred Stanfield to Boston. Stanfield had been one of my best friends throughout my early career, but that wasn't what made the trade so bad. It was the fact that Boston, with whom Bobby Orr had just played his rookie year, now had a supporting cast for Orr to play with. It made Boston an overnight contender for the Stanley Cup.

After Fred left for Boston, we didn't see each other much during the season. Because of that, we often got together when the hockey year had ended. On one occasion, we went to Acapulco on vacation. We were in a villa and it turned out the Esposito brothers were also staying at the resort. Freddie was a party waiting to happen. His talent was drinking all night, but no one would ever know he'd been drinking. It didn't appear to have any effect on him. On the second night, he told me we were staying up all night and he proceeded to make a jug of vodka and grapefruit juice.

In the middle of the night, as we were sitting in the sand by the pool, hundreds of sand crabs appeared and ran across the sand.

"Let's get some of those," Freddie said, grabbing a shoe box. We stuffed the box full of crabs and plopped the lid on it.

It was at this point that Freddie remembered the Espositos were petrified of anything that crawled. It didn't matter whether it was a fly or spider or, in this case, a crab. They were simply terrified of anything built close to the ground. It was like an elephant seeing a mouse.

"Come on, Dennis," Freddie said, heading towards the Espositos' door. He knocked on the door at 4 AM.

"Who is it?" Phil asked.

"It's me," Freddie said, "and when you come to the door, remember there's nothing in the shoe box."

It was the first time I could tell he'd been drinking.

Orr was dominant even as a rookie, when he played on a terrible team. He'd try to do everything himself and he almost could. The year Orr broke in, Harry Howell, who played with the Rangers, won the Norris Trophy. I still remember Howell being quoted as saying it was nice to win the award because nobody except for Bobby Orr was going to win it for the next ten years. When Tommy Ivan decided to trade Esposito, Hodge, and Stanfield to Boston, all of a sudden Orr was on a contender.

Given that trade, I'm surprised Tommy Ivan was kept on as general manager. In fact, he's still with the Blackhawks, even though he's in his mid-80s, because in 1961, when the Blackhawks won the Cup, James Norris Jr., the owner at the time, gave him a lifetime job. I guess nobody thought that meant he would stay with the team his entire lifetime!

One of the other problems with the trade was that Bobby and Phil Esposito got along very well. Up until this point, Bobby's line was always Bobby and whoever else was available. I still think that Bobby was the most exciting player to ever put on a pair of skates. However, if you think about Gordie Howe, fans and players alike think about his linemates, Ted Lindsay and Sid Abel, or Al Delvecchio and Lindsay. If you think about Maurice Richard you think about Toe Blake and Elmer Lach.

I ask people who they think of when they think of Bobby Hull and the answer is always the same. Nobody. He never played with anyone. It was just whoever was left over. Stan Mikita and Bobby couldn't play together because they both had to have the puck all the time. It was tried, but didn't work. He needed someone like Chico Maki, who would provide the defensive side. Bobby could simply do it all. He was one of the fastest players in the league and had his big shot. With the blond hair flowing, he was a favourite everywhere in the league.

Other teams in Chicago at the time, the Bears and the Cubs, had stars too. The Bears had Sayers and Butkus. The Cubs had Banks and Santo. Bobby was the biggest sports star though. He couldn't walk around Toronto or Montreal without being mobbed.

The Blackhawks would go into New York and the sign would say, "Bobby Hull and the rest of the Blackhawks against the Rangers." He was sort of like the Michael Jordan of his day. Before Bobby came into the league, most goals were scored close to the net with a wrist shot. A player wasn't dangerous outside the blue line. But Bobby could shoot so hard that he *was* dangerous anywhere. That filtered down, and ten years later, everybody slapped the puck like Bobby. It's amazing how individuals can change the game. For ten years he was hockey. He took it from shirtsleeves and put it into a tie.

With Esposito, Bobby finally had someone who complimented his game. It was perfect, but it didn't last. Maybe the Blackhawks traded Phil because he was a little different than the rest of the players. Esposito was such a free spirit. He loved the Three Stooges. He could do all the routines. But I think the Blackhawks thought he was a bit flakey.

I'd played Junior with Phil, so I knew what he was like. Once, while playing the Marlboros in Maple Leaf Gardens, he had the puck and was singing while he came by our bench.

The big song of the day had lyrics like, "What's your name? Is it Mary or Sue?" And here was Esposito singing the song at the top of his lungs.

Before he started on Bobby's line, he didn't play much. I remember a game in Toronto in 1965, when we were down 5–1, Billy Reay sent him out on the ice. He took four strides, turned around, and skated back toward the bench.

"What you want me to do?" he said to Reay. "Win it or tie it?"

I thought I was going to play the rest of my career with Fred, and when Ken joined the team, everything seemed perfect. We were all 20. I thought we'd play until we were 35. I heard about the trade on the radio. I couldn't believe it. The Hawks got Pit Martin and Gilles Marotte, but that didn't make it an even trade.

Martin was one of two guys the Blackhawks' management thought would end up playing with Bobby. The other was Jimmy Pappin, a right winger who had played with Toronto. Martin was fast and could keep up with Bobby, and Jimmy was a great playmaker, so Billy figured he could set Bobby up. The two were a perfect fit for Bobby.

The problem was that in 1968, when they came to training camp, Bobby was holding out in a contract dispute. We went to start the first game of the season and Billy had to decide who would play with Jimmy and Pit.

"Dennis, you'll play with Jimmy and Pit until Bobby gets back," he told me before the game.

Those few games lasted eight years. Despite the fact Pit and Jimmy were intended as Bobby's linemates, it was clear from the start that they were going to end up playing with me. Bobby was out five games, but we got three goals the first game and two goals the next game. It was decided that we would stay together, forming the MPH line.

Bobby came back and once more played with whoever was left on the bench. So I even got my linemates because of Bobby. But Bobby didn't really need special players.

It was clear it was going to be easy to become friends with both Jimmy and Pit. Jimmy was a good player, but he kept being sent down when he was with Toronto. In 1967, when the Leafs won the Stanley Cup, Pappin was the best player in the series. Dave

Keon received the Conn Smythe, but Pappin played better.

He was also smarter about hockey than anyone I played with. He was naturally adept at it. Jimmy led me along, and without my linemates, I'd never have scored 300 goals.

Pit was not as clever on the ice as Jimmy, but had great speed and forechecking abilities. It's funny, though, because Jimmy would yell and scream at the two of us during the games. I didn't resent it; to the contrary, I found that Jimmy motivated me to play better. If someone told me what to do, I could always do it and Jimmy played that role. With Billy cajoling me, and Jimmy screaming at me, I think I got more out of my limited abilities than anyone thought possible. Jimmy would get so intense that I remember seeing him slash Pit for failing to pass the puck to me on a two-on-one break. He also yelled at Pit so much that Billy had me sit between the two of them on the bench. But as soon as we got off the ice, he was a different person.

When Bobby came back, they wanted Pit to play with Bobby, so they moved him back on the line. But it just didn't work; they simply couldn't play together. On top of this he was having problems with his wife. I saw him soon after and he looked miserable.

"What's wrong, Pit?"

"God, nothing's going right," he said. "Playing with Bobby isn't working and then there's the problems with my wife."

He paused for a moment and thought about his situation.

"You know what would work?" he commented. "If I found Bobby with my wife I could shoot them both and my problems would be over."

With that he laughed, and soon after he was put back onto a line with Jimmy and myself.

Pit and Jimmy were both outgoing and we always had fun after the games. A few years after we started playing together, we were caught by Billy after curfew in Philadelphia. We'd tied the game 5–5 on a Sunday night and didn't have to play again until Wednesday. Most of the team went down to the hotel bar, which we weren't supposed to do. I think Billy knew we were there but wasn't too concerned about it.

However, at 1 AM he received a call from someone complaining about all the players that were drinking. Now he felt he had to do something, so he threw on some clothes and went down to the bar. The elevator was a little ways down the hall in the hotel, and once we saw Billy we knew there was no escape. Some guys were caught at the door, but Pit and I ran into the kitchen. I tried to convince Pit to go into the dumb waiter, but he wouldn't do it. Eventually we waited until enough time had passed that Billy would have left.

We walked out the kitchen door and there was Billy looking right at us.

The next day we went to Montreal and Billy called a meeting for 6 PM. We knew we were going to catch hell. Billy had even cancelled our reservation at the Mount Royal Hotel and taken us to some hole in the wall.

Billy opened the meeting. "Pinder, what do you think of this place I've got you in?"

"Well, it's very nice, Sir," Pinder said.

"No, it's not, Pinder. It's second class, just like you, Pinder!"

That was the start of a rant where he screamed at every player. I was at the end of his list.

"Dennis, I didn't think you were anything like Bobby, but after midnight, you're just the same!"

From out of nowhere Jimmy chimed in.

"Well, coach, if that's the case, do you think we can schedule some later games?"

That was the end of the meeting.

In Billy's system, if you started a game and won, then you started the next game. Billy Reay always rewarded the players who were doing well. And the MPH line soon became one of the dominant lines on the Blackhawks, scoring 83 goals our first year together.

But I used to like giving Billy a hard time.

"How come the line's always named after the centre?" I asked Billy, who always referred to our line as the Martin line. "I want it to be named after me!"

"Well, you're not getting a line named after you," he said, as he walked away from me shaking his head.

*I*n 1968, the Democratic National Convention was held in Chicago. There were street riots during the convention and the police received a lot of bad press for their role in the mess. Due to the problems they'd had, the police were under orders to be pro-active. They even stopped people and gave them safe driving citations. It was a strange era.

At the time, there was a rule in hockey that if a player was with the team after December 15, the team couldn't send him to the minors until January 15. It was put in place so players wouldn't have their holidays disrupted. Doug and I never knew if we'd make it past December 15, so when we didn't get sent down, we'd go out and celebrate.

In 1968 we had passed the deadline so we went out and were over-served in a downtown Chicago bar. We were coming back and Doug, who was trying to be inconspicuous, was driving the back streets towards the expressway. He was doing a good job, stopping at all the signs and indicating lane changes. However, despite his good driving, we still managed to get pulled over by a policeman.

"Just relax," the cop said. "I've been following you for the last mile and it's two in the morning and you've signalled, stopped for every stop sign, and done everything perfectly."

Doug looked at him and said, "When you're as drunk as we are, you've got to be careful."

I was asleep by the time he got out of the police car. It cost him two season tickets to get out of that jam.

ELEVEN

The Prankster

*I*n 1965, Pat Stapleton joined the Blackhawks, coming over from Boston. Pat was a great player, having won the Memorial Cup in 1960 playing on a terrific team which included Ray Cullen, Vic Hadfield, and Roger Crozier, but off the ice he created chaos. Without a doubt, he was the number one practical joker on Chicago, and may have been the best in the league. He was unbelievable.

It began soon after he arrived. There had been a little scandal about horse race fixing in Chicago and Billy Reay had a horse. Pat put the connection together and had a friend, dressed like an FBI officer, come into the dressing room.

Billy was talking when this guy walked in. No one ever came into our meetings, so Billy seemed astounded that this man had simply walked in.

"What are you doing here?" Billy asked.

The guy flashed an FBI badge and took Billy out of the room. He told Billy about the horse scandal and told him he would be watched closely.

It wasn't until much later in the day that Billy found out what Stapleton had done. He wasn't pleased and told Pat. "If we lose tonight," he said, "I'm sending you home."

In the game that night Pat played like I'd never seen him play before and we managed to win. I'm pretty certain Billy would have followed through on his threat, so it's a good thing for Pat that he turned it on.

On another occasion, in 1968, we were going to Minnesota from Chicago and the referees were on the same flight. The officials always carried their own skates instead of checking them just to make sure there wouldn't be a problem. On this flight Bill Friday had his skates with him. Pat, being devious, took Friday's skates and hid them with the stewardesses. Friday looked all over and couldn't find them, but he knew of Stapleton's reputation and figured it was him.

Pat kept the skates until just before the game had started. In the meantime, Friday had already received another pair of skates from the North Stars. Finally the trainer took Friday his skates, but the game was held up for a few minutes while Friday put them on.

He came out and dropped the puck at centre ice. The puck came back to Stapleton and a Minnesota guy came toward him. Friday blew the whistle.

"Stapleton," he said. "You've got two minutes."

The problem was that Billy didn't know about the stunt.

"What's going on?" Billy yelled. "He never even went near him and he's got two minutes?"

I was always very careful around Pat, but his roommate in the 1967 season, Ed Van Impe, wasn't as lucky. During that season, we were in Boston and heard that Elizabeth Taylor was going to check into the hotel, so we waited for her. I was standing at the back of the lobby with the guys who were talking to Elizabeth Taylor, but I could see Pat talking to the bellboy. I knew something was up.

The next day I found out Stapleton had told the bellboy that he was a pilot for United Airlines and that his fellow pilot, Ed Van Impe, had missed his last two flights. He said if Van Impe missed another flight, he was going to lose his job.

He then proceeded to tell the bellboy to look after Van Impe that night and slipped the bellboy $10.

"I want you to makes sure he gets up," he told the guy. "His flight's at 7 AM and he has to get up by 5 AM."

Pat told the bellboy that the reason Van Impe missed the flights was that he loved to sleep and he'd lie and do anything to stay in bed. With this in mind, the bell boy came up at 4:45 AM, opened the door and came in.

Ed jumped up and said, "What's the matter?"

"Well, come on, Mr. Van Impe, you've got to catch your flight."

"I don't have to catch any flight."

"Oh yes you do," the bell boy said, thinking Ed was lying to him. "Come on or you'll lose your job as a pilot with United."

"But I play with the Chicago Blackhawks!"

"Oh come on. Stop the lies," the bellboy said.

All the while Pat was killing himself trying not to laugh.

But Pat wasn't through with Ed. Another time we were in New York playing the Rangers when Pat pulled off another trick.

The old hotels in New York had radiators and when they'd come on they'd make a rattling and hissing sound. When we checked in, Pat noticed it and devised a plan.

We were having our pre-game meal when I overheard Pat talking to Ed.

"There's a bomber in New York," Stapleton said authoritatively, "and he's blown up a couple of hotels. And there's only been one survivor. The survivor said that there was only one thing he could remember: just before the bomb went off there was a rattling noise and a hissing."

Eddie was gullible, I guess, because he went right along with the story and looked really concerned.

They went up to their room that afternoon and the rads were off, but when they came back on they rattled and hissed. Pat said Eddie was in hallway as fast as he could possibly go.

"What about me?" Pat yelled at Eddie. "Are you going to leave me here with the bomb?"

Later in the season I got a chance to talk to Ed about rooming with Pat.

"It's great being Pat's roommate," Van Impe said, "because this way my wife tells me what to do at home and Pat tells me what to do on the road."

*T*he only time the Blackhawks missed the playoffs in my career was in 1968–69. But we managed to turn it around and finish at the top of the East Division in 1969–70. It was the first time a team had ever gone from last to first in one year. The only real difference in the team between the two years was Tony Esposito, Phil's brother, whom we'd acquired in a trade with Montreal. Montreal had Esposito and a newcomer named Ken Dryden in the wings, and the Canadiens decided to go with Dryden. Denis DeJordy had been our netminder for much of the late 1960s, but he was never a strong NHL goalie. Tony had 15 shutouts in his first full year, won the Calder Trophy, we finished in first.

Though we ended up in first place, the year finished strangely in a game against Montreal. The Habs were facing their first playoff elimination in 22 years, and even though they were tied with New York for points, they needed to have more goals scored in order to finish ahead of the Rangers. The problem was that the Rangers were up by six goals.

I noticed something odd was up when Montreal began pulling their goalie early in the game in order to get a sixth skater. It never crossed my mind that the Canadiens might try a stunt like this, but it made sense. After all, they didn't have to win the game, they just had to score six goals. Despite pulling the goalie, it failed. However, I never did see our guys move as quickly to get the puck as they did that night!

The funny thing about Tony's success was that Phil had no problem scoring on Tony. There was no tension between them, it's just that Phil had taken more shots against Tony than anyone else and had him figured out.

Every player has a nemesis. Mine was Johnny Bower. He was an angle goalie and he'd always cut off my shots. However, I always had good luck against Ken Dryden, so it wasn't necessarily the good goalies that caused me problems.

There were also goalies who became afraid of facing shots from Bobby and me. The Flyers' Bernie Parent was a great goalie, but whenever we played Philadelphia, he didn't play. Guys on the Flyers used to say he had No. 9 fever. He was simply petrified of Bobby.

Likewise, when we played in Montreal, Rogie Vachon, their goalie in the late sixties, used to hang around to watch us practise.

There was a time when Billy approached me and Bobby, knowing Vachon was watching.

"Hey Dennis, Bobby. Fire a bunch high and off the crossbar," he said. "Shoot them off the glass."

This guy would sit there and watch Bobby and me fire shot after shot at 100 miles an hour. They'd fly off the cross bar and off the end plexiglass. You could see the colour start to drain from Vachon's face. He'd started to shake when he finally walked away.

Getting Bobby and me to fire high shots was a practice Billy employed regularly in games. He'd come up and say, "Fire a couple high." It would keep the opposing goalie on his toes.

Goalies began to get used to the shooting style of Bobby and me. Gerry Cheevers, who played goal for the Bruins, was one of the most adept at dealing with the Hull shot. I was never the most gifted puck handler, but because of my shot, there were lots of times when I'd be cruising over the red line and I'd put my head down and shoot. There's a great picture of me shooting the puck at Gerry, except rather than being in the net, he's out near the blue line. That's because he knew once I'd teed it up I was going to let it fly.

I once hit Ranger goalie Ed Giacomin with one of these shots. Giacomin may have been the most precise goalie I ever played against, but in this case, he couldn't deal with a deflected shot which flew up and hit him right in the mask. Because I was skating hard across the Rangers' blue line, I was the first one to reach Giacomin. When the trainer took the plastic mask off, Giacomin was out cold. But I remember noticing that where the air holes in the mask were, he had little marks on his face, almost like he had measles.

Once the trainer revived him, Plante looked around and saw the Rangers' Rod Gilbert, and said, "I told you that you were not supposed to let him shoot."

TWELVE

The Stolen Car

On November 6, 1966, Sue and I had our first child, a daughter whom we named Martha. While current athletes are allowed to go and be with their wives when they have a baby, that wasn't the case in the sixties. Martha was born while I was on the road in Boston. We were having our pre-game meal when Billy Reay called me aside and said, "Son, you're now a father." I scored a goal that night and kept the puck and gave it to my daughter when she was older.

Sue and I loved our daughter so much that another girl would have been all right with us. In 1968, Sue got pregnant again. The delivery was in Chicago and I was hanging around in the "heirport," the name for the waiting room at the hospital, to see the baby.

The nurse finally came out and had a baby in her arms.

"Mr. Hull, this is yours," she said, presenting me with the baby.

"But is it a boy or a girl?"

She lifted the blanket up.

"Well, look at the plumbing on this guy!" she said.

That was my son John, who's lived up to that billing ever since.

*M*y wife almost never went to see me play hockey, which in the end was probably just as well. When we first met, she went to a few Junior games, but I consider it fortunate that I found someone who didn't want to be with a hockey player. She cared whether I won or lost, but it didn't affect her life with me.

However, Sue didn't even have a passing interest in coming to see me play in Chicago because of the way I was treated by the fans. She said she didn't like the names they yelled at me, so it was easier if she didn't go.

From 1964 to 1970, she never went to a game. I'd meet her after the game and we'd go out, but she never actually came to the games.

One Sunday afternoon in 1970, we had a disagreement. It turned into a big argument. At 5 PM I was getting ready to go to the stadium and Sue began to get her coat on.

"Where are you going?" I asked.

"I'm going to the hockey game."

"But you haven't been to a hockey game in six years. Why are you going now?"

"Because I want to be with 20,000 other people who feel exactly the same way I do about you."

*I*n 1971, we finished first in the division again and began to make a run for the Cup. I scored 40 goals that season and Bobby netted 44. Bobby was playing so well that he probably could have scored 100 goals, but he was hooked and grabbed all the time. I remember talking to referee Bill Friday about it.

"Come on Bill," I said, "there's a penalty every minute against Bobby."

"But he's better than they are," was the response.

Our aim on the team was always the same; we wanted to play through the World Series, then through the Super Bowl and the

Kentucky Derby. Finally, we wanted to be playing when the Masters was on. In order to play through the Masters, you had to play in the Stanley Cup. I remember that year that I was having a good string of luck. There was a pool for the Kentucky Derby and I drew the field. In other words, I drew all the losers. But I won. The Preakness, I drew the field again and won again. Luck was with me.

The funny thing was that Billy was tricking everyone. In 1971, the MPH line had 84 goals among us. Billy made sure that nobody thought the best line in Chicago was Martin-Pappin-Hull. He always said the best players were Stan Mikita and Bobby Hull.

"If you stop those two guys you stop the Blackhawks," he said, time and again.

A few years ago Ted Irvine, who was scouting for the Rangers at the time, came up to me at a game.

"You know what I've figured out? Billy Reay screwed us for all those years. He was telling everyone that the best players were Stan Mikita and Bobby, and you guys would score 100 goals! How can a third line score that many?"

But it was deception on Billy's part to keep the other teams from putting their best lines against us.

We beat Philadelphia in the first round of the playoffs that year before meeting the Rangers in the semi-finals. It was during a game in that series when I silenced Madison Square Garden with one shot. Rangers' defenceman Harry Howell was in the penalty box when I got the puck; I wound up and shot it up the boards. But it went over the boards and looked like it hit Harry Howell in the head. He went right down on the floor of the penalty box, so you couldn't see him.

The Garden went quiet and everyone was watching the box.

Slowly, Howell's stick came up and at the top was a white towel. He'd surrendered.

During the series, the coaches had told the players not to say anything controversial to the press and to always say nice things about the opposing players. New York had taken two of the first three games in the series. After we won the fourth game, Vic Hadfield said, "We had to let them win one."

That got us fired up, and we eliminated the Rangers in seven games.

As the playoffs went along, it was clear I had a chance at the Conn Smythe trophy as most valuable player during the playoffs. I had a good series against Philly and then, following my play against New York, which went seven games, every time we won, Jimmy or Pit or Bobby would give me a piece of the car you were given for winning the trophy. They'd give me the ash tray and then the steering wheel and then the front seat. As it turned out, although I was the leading scorer on the team and the league through the playoffs, a rookie would take the trophy away from me.

The Stanley Cup came down to a matchup of the Blackhawks against the Canadiens yet again. There were a number of long-term rivalries between the teams. The battles went back a long way. When I first started playing in Montreal, Maurice "Rocket" Richard had already retired, but he'd still come to every game and sit over the exit to the dressing rooms. He liked to taunt Bobby.

"Hey Bobby — one day you'll be ugly and fat, just like me," he yelled.

However, none of these rivalries was as heated as the feud between Stan Mikita and "The Pocket Rocket," Henri Richard.

Stan was as good as Wayne Gretzky with the puck, but in order to get an image of what Stan was like as a player, you have to imagine Gretzky also hacking people and spearing opponents. Stan and Henri Richard just didn't get along. Every game they'd hack and spear one another and bicker back and forth. They didn't dislike one another — it was more of a hatred. After these incidents, when they were both sitting in the penalty box, I liked to go over to hear them scream at each other. It was the worst stuff you could imagine.

There was a time when Henri was getting into the penalty box after an incident with Stan. Henri was shaking because he was so angry. He saw me skating over and said, "What's the matter with that stupid D.P.?" in reference to Stan being a "displaced person" or immigrant. Before I could answer, Henri yelled, "He can't even speak the good English!"

Because of the battles between Henri and Stan, Maurice always hated Mikita as well. We'd be heading off between periods after Stan and Henri had one of their jousts and The Rocket would sit in his perch and yell at Mikita. Stan would just egg him on.

"Hey Dennis, watch this," Stan said to me during the second intermission of a game in Montreal. I followed Stan off and when he saw the Rocket he began taunting him.

"Hey you old has-been."

This always made the Rocket go crazy.

"If I was out there I'd kill you," Rocket yelled. "Don't you touch my brother again."

Stan stood there for a minute and then took his stick and tipped Maurice's beer all over him, which only made him more infuriated. Then we walked into the dressing room.

Maurice only yelled at the stars, people who approached his level. He's still crusty and I see him occasionally. For a while, we both played in a golf tournament together, but suddenly Maurice stopped showing up.

"Henri, I brought my brother, why didn't you bring your brother?"

"Well, I brought him last year and he bounced a cheque for $5,000," he answered.

Like Stan, Henri was one of the greatest competitors I ever encountered in hockey, despite being a very quiet guy. When Toe Blake came to Montreal, he approached one of the players in order to get a sense of the team.

"Does Henri Richard speak English?" Blake asked.

"I don't even know if he speaks French," was the reply.

In a strange way, the great rivalry we had with the Canadiens brought us closer to them than other teams we played. I knew each of the players inside and out.

In every game we played against one another, Henri always did the same thing. He'd get behind me and mutter in his thick accent, "My brudder is bedder dan your brudder."

It used to make me laugh. A few years ago we were playing in an oldtimers' game and he did his routine about how The Rocket was better than Bobby. But I was prepared.

"Well, my nephew is better than your brother," I said.

"Well, maybe," came the reply.

When we were playing the fifth game against Montreal, Stapleton took a puck in the face and had to have forty stitches, which was pretty serious. We were going to Montreal to play the sixth game and Leo Durocher, the manager of the Cubs at the time, came up to me and Jimmy Pappin as we were getting ready to get on the plane at O'Hare airport.

"That's too bad about Stapleton," Durocher said. "You guys would have had a chance to win this."

"What are you talking about," Pappin said. "Pat's right over there and he's not out."

"He's going to play tomorrow?" Durocher questioned.

"Why not?" Jimmy said. "He's just got a cut on his face."

"One of my guys would be out for two years if that happened to him," Durocher said. "Well if Pat Stapleton can play tomorrow, I'm going to get kicked out of the ball game and come to watch."

And if you check the statistics in both baseball and hockey, you'll see that we played the sixth game in Montreal and Durocher got kicked out of the Cubs–Expos afternoon game in the first inning. And I remember seeing him watching the game that night at the Forum.

The other unusual thing that happened during the sixth game in Montreal was that Henri decided it would be an appropriate time to criticize the Canadiens' coach, Al MacNeil. He said MacNeil was the worst coach in the history of the game. For that comment, MacNeil sat Richard out of the sixth game. But in the seventh game, Henri was back.

The series was very close, and we were ahead 3–2. It's funny how people think the playoffs are all life or death and nothing funny ever happens. In the sixth game I went into the corner with Yvan Cournoyer, Jacques Lemaire, and Serge Savard. In this melee I stepped on the puck and cleared everyone. We were lying in a pile and the lineman, Leon Stickle, came down and picked up the puck.

"Wrong wax boys," he said, which cracked us up.

We dropped the sixth game, 4–3, forcing a final game.

During our morning skate the day of the seventh game, Bob Verdi, who wrote for the *Chicago Tribune* and travelled with the team, polled a bunch of reporters about who they thought would win the Conn Smythe trophy. Verdi was an interesting guy — he hung out with us all the time and never reported anything we did away from the rink. Of course this was the era when players had lives outside the public's gaze. His poll indicated that if we won the series, I would win the Conn Smythe trophy and, if we lost, Ken Dryden was going to win it.

The trophy had drawn some controversy over the years, generally because a Montreal player hadn't won it, even when the team took the Cup.

The Canadiens didn't get it in 1966 because it was given to Roger Crozier of Detroit for his amazing play, despite a last-minute goal by Henri Richard that might have warranted it being awarded to him. A couple of years later, Montreal won in four straight against St. Louis in 1968, but Glenn Hall got the trophy.

I think following that, it was decided that a player on the winning team would get the trophy. The day before the game, the team received a telegram stating each player could invite two people to the Stanley Cup party if we won. Our dressing room was also filled with television cables, so the camera crews would be prepared to show the celebrations if we won.

I scored our first goal and Dan O'Shea scored the second at the 12-minute mark. Up 2–0, Pit Martin gave Jimmy Pappin a pass. Pappin had the whole net open and fired the puck. He knew he'd scored so he threw his hands up in the air. The only problem was that Dryden stopped it. The next minute, Bobby was in all alone and hit the cross bar.

We were still leading 2–1 going into the third period when we had a bad line change; Keith Magnuson was rushing to his position and Henri Richard went around him and scored. And then Richard scored again, putting us down by a goal, which turned out to be the winner.

It was heartbreaking, because we were so close. In the next couple of years, I would've taken the loss to the Soviets in exchange for that game and a chance to have beaten the Canadiens. I played my whole career trying to win a Stanley Cup and we never did. When we went to play the Russians, it was all new. Nobody knew then how much it mattered in the scheme of things. But I would have traded the '72 Series for a Stanley Cup.

After the loss to the Canadiens, there were no cameras, no interviews. I remember Henri skating around the ice with the Stanley Cup for the eleventh time.

One of my other brothers, Ron, and I went out and had a few beers. There was no celebration. Over the summer, everyone came up to me and said, "You were the better team." But it didn't matter because we didn't win.

The next fall, our first exhibition game was in Ottawa against the Canadiens. It was like the season had never stopped. In this exhibition game Cournoyer came up to me.

"Hey Dennis," he said.

"Yeah, what do you want?"

"I got a message from Dryden. He says your car is running real good."

With a friend in Pointe Anne.
What a great place to grow up!

One of the July 1st family boot-
and-shoe races in Pointe Anne.

Rod Turner (front row, second from left, next to me) and Stuart Muirhead (third
from right) were two of my best friends. They lived in Belleville and let me stay
at their houses on Friday nights, saving me that six-mile walk back to Pointe Anne.

My dad (third from left) as foreman of the cement plant in Pointe Anne. As he said at the time, "The working class can kiss my ass, I've got a foreman's job at last!"

In front of the cement plant in 1954, in my first jacket (a hand-me-down from Garry).

One of the Hull houses in Pointe Anne. When my dad got promoted we got a better house.

With my friend Stuart Muirhead, hanging out on a lazy summer day in Pointe Anne.

My first hockey photo. Even then I posed like an NHLer.

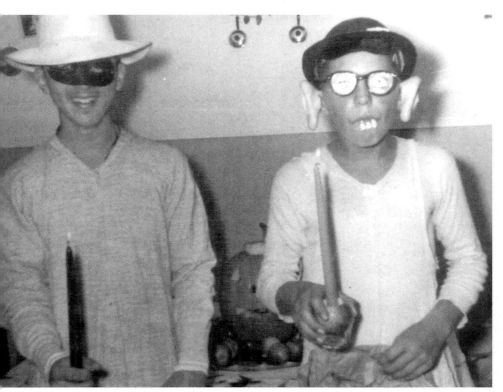

My friend Peter Everett and I go trick-or-treating, 1958.

My grade nine class picture, from
Quinte Secondary School in Belleville.

A studio portrait I had done
right before going to the NHL.

Doug Jarrett and I in our last year of Junior. Doug
was MVP and I was voted Most Popular Player.
(I should have told that to the fans in Chicago!)

The players' door at Chicago
Stadium. I was now a Blackhawk

Two early shots of me as a rookie
on the Chicago Blackhawks.

No, it's not Bobby in the #9. That's me as a junior playing against the Marlies.

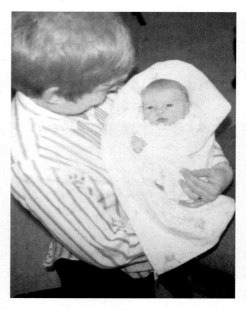

Sue's parents, Molly and John Newman. They lived and died with every game.

Sue with our daughter Martha, the love of our life.

Sue and I with Mom in our first home together. There would be 20 more.

Dad and I before
a game at the
Montreal Forum.

My dad with Brian McFarlane, probably telling h
he taught Bobby and I everything we know.

BLACK HAWKS

DENNIS HULL *forward*

DENNIS HULL

DENNIS HULL LEFT WING
CHICAGO BLACK HAWKS

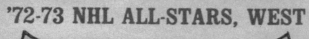

'72-73 NHL ALL-STARS, WEST

LEFT WING   BLACK HAWKS

☆   **DENNIS HULL**   ☆

DENNIS HULL   CHICAGO FORWARD

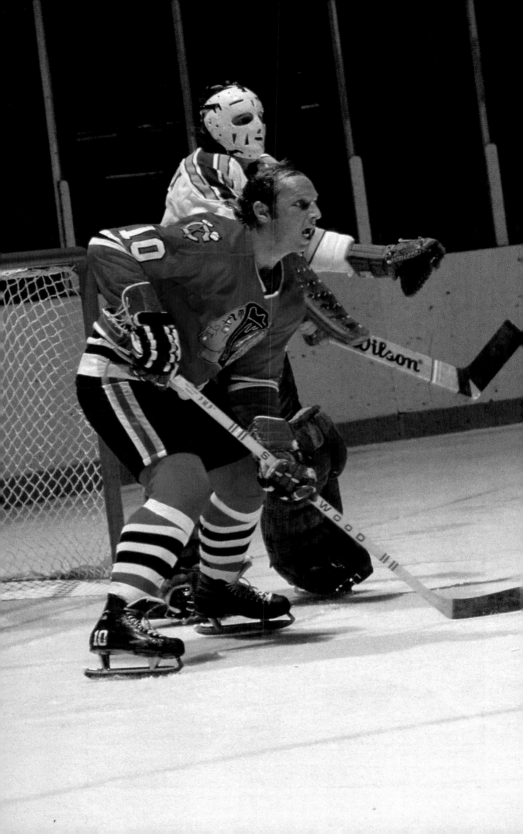

The MPH line: me, Pit Martin, and Jim Pappin. These guys are two of the best friends a person could have. *Inset:* The MPH line with less hair.

I was never as happy
in a Wings' uniform.

THIRTEEN

I'll Flip You for It

*W*e finished first again in 1971–72 and it looked like we might make it back to the Stanley Cup. Bobby and I had 80 goals combined that year, 30 of which were mine. It was during the first-round series against Pittsburgh, which we won in four straight, that the league officials first decided to measure the blade of a hockey stick.

The invention of the curved stick blade rests solely with Stan Mikita and the fact that the Chicago Stadium had twenty-two steps a player needed to walk down to get to the dressing room. One day during a practice, Stan broke the blade of his stick lengthwise from the end of the blade to the shaft. Because of this, the blade curled. Stan sent the trainer to get another stick, but as it took the trainer a while to trudge up and down the stairs, Stan continued to play with the broken stick. He found you could get the puck off the ice much quicker with the bent blade. After his discovery, all the players were trying to bend their sticks, stepping on them and wedging them in doors. At one point, there was such a bend in the blade of my stick that you couldn't see the puck when I was skating down the ice.

By 1970, the league had decided to do something about this and put a rule in place to limit the amount of bend a player could

have on the blade of his stick. The rule was never really enforced
though. But when league president Clarence Campbell and
Dutch VanDeelen who was the head of the officials, both showed
up for one of the playoff games in Pittsburgh, we knew something was up.

With three minutes left in the game, John Ashley, the referee
for the game, came over to Jim Pappin to check his stick.

Ashley went to get the stick and Pappin turned and threw
it into the stands, knowing it would be ruled illegal. Ashley
promptly gave Pappin two minutes for unsportsmanlike conduct.
Pappin got out of the box, got another stick and Ashley came
over again. This time Pappin stepped on his stick, breaking the
blade. Ashley gave him another two-minute penalty. I was standing on the ice laughing — I'd never seen anything like it. All of
a sudden, Ashley grabbed my stick and measured it with the
device they had to check the sticks. Of course it was illegal. The
first stick ever ruled illegal.

In the oldtimer's games we still measure sticks by putting them
up to Eddie Shack's nose. That way, they're always legal.

After getting by the Penguins, we took on the New York
Rangers in a rematch from the previous year. It was also during
that series that Billy devised the non-speaking team spokesman.
Billy hated New York, and especially the press that hounded him.
In the semi-final in 1972, he said nobody could talk to the press
in New York. The press were really angry about it and com-
plained, so the NHL said someone had to deal with the media.
That's when Billy hit a stroke of genius and told J.P. Bordeleau,
a rookie who had lived all his life in Quebec, that he could act as
the club spokesman.

There were two problems, however. The first was that Billy
designated J.P. Bordeleau because he could only speak broken
English and the press wouldn't be able to understand much of
what he said. The second problem was that J.P. had only played
three games in the season that year and hardly made it onto
the ice during the playoffs. The press wasn't very happy about the

outcome, but J.P. was sure happy to be the centre of attention. After every game I'd see him grinning from ear to ear as all the press gathered around to hear what he had to say about the game.

Throughout my time with Chicago, the players almost always went to the same places, especially since most of us lived in Hillside, a Chicago suburb. We always ate at Stimac's. Stimac's was a restaurant that we went to mainly because we knew we wouldn't be bothered. Only locals went. You were just like one of the regulars. And the players always knew that if the game was late, Joe Stimac, the owner, would always make you a burger.

Unfortunately, we dropped the series to New York in four straight. Following the last game, which was on a Saturday night, the team made a retreat to Stimac's. We got there knowing we weren't going to play the next day, which was Easter Sunday. It was a very down time, and probably would have been more depressing had we known that Bobby had just played his last game as a Blackhawk.

The team was looking to drink a lot of beer, so out it came. Soon it was two in the morning. By the time we looked up next it was four. By the time seven rolled around, Joe went and made breakfast.

Now it was Easter Sunday, which most of us had forgotten about, and by 11 in the morning we were still there. Then we had lunch. A night of drinking beer hadn't left us in very good shape.

Just as we were starting lunch, my daughter, who was two at the time, walked in with an Easter bonnet on.

She grabbed me by the hand.

"Can you come home now, Daddy?"

So we left.

*T*he off-season in 1972 was a very strange time. By 1972 it was clear that a new league, which became the World Hockey Association, was going to start up to rival the NHL.

The fact is that the NHL had it easy for a long time.

My first contract was for $7,500. That was the minimum and I received a $1,500 bonus to sign, which was a step up from Junior, where I'd made $60 a week. Since Doug and I lived together in Junior, and paid $50 a month rent combined between the two of us, that didn't seem like a poor wage.

We knew the owners were making a lot of money, but the players deserved a portion of it. The problem was that the only thing most players knew how to do was play hockey. Guys used to say they were going to hold out and go home and work, and management always said that was fine, knowing the player was likely to return.

Where were they going to work? In a factory?

And without a Players' Association, which didn't form until 1967, there weren't many choices for players. Few players could do what they wanted — Glenn Hall retired, or threatened to retire every year, but he simply couldn't make as much money farming as he could playing goal.

Of course the guy who looked after our Players' Association, Alan Eagleson, turned out to be a criminal. But we didn't know that at the time. In 1967, he came into the dressing room to give his speech on the reasons that he should be the head of the Players' Association. After he left the dressing room, Bobby got up and talked to the team.

"This guy is a crook," Bobby said.

But everyone defended Eagleson. He was Bobby Orr's agent, after all. It went to a vote and I decided I would stick with Bobby. The vote was 18–2.

Eagleson aside, one of the problems was the treatment of Gordie Howe by the Detroit management. When he played for Detroit, the team's management would simply dictate what his salary would be. It held salaries down for quite a while, because if you went in and said you wanted to make $50,000, the general manager would say, "Are you crazy? Gordie Howe is only making $40,000."

And that was a hard point to argue. After all, he was Mr. Hockey and all the other players seemed something less when compared to him.

The story broke after expansion, when people got traded around. In 1967 Bobby Baun was lost in the Expansion Draft to Oakland and then was shuttled off to Detroit.

"It's embarrassing," he said to me. "I go to Detroit and I'm making more than Gordie Howe."

My brother had held out a couple of times, but he had nowhere to go, and GM Tommy Ivan was always tough when it came to negotiations.

In the mid-sixties, Ivan once offered left-winger Reggie Fleming $7,000. Fleming was a little confused and asked Ivan if the salary being offered was a bit too low. "Mr. Ivan, the minimum is $7,500," he said.

"Well, we've got to start somewhere," Ivan replied.

I always thought that Ivan was given a certain amount of money to sign the players and if he came in with a lower figure, he would get to keep what was left over.

My experiences with Ivan started when I began to score a lot of goals. I went into his office at the start of the year in 1971, the season after I'd scored 40 goals.

"I don't want you on this team and the fans don't want you on this team," he said. "Nobody wants you on this team. The only person who wants you on this team is Billy Reay."

"But Mr. Ivan, I just scored 40 goals," I said, kind of dumbstruck.

"I don't care," was his response. He told me I was being greedy, which made me defensive.

"Now Mr. Ivan, I don't want anything more that any other 40-goal scorer gets. That's all I want."

"Do you mean that?"

"Absolutely."

"I'm going to get the contracts of all the other 40-goal scorers and I'll give you the average," he said.

"Well, that's all right by me."

The next day he came back and called me into his office again.

"You tricked me, didn't you?" he questioned.

I didn't know what he was talking about. It turned out the only 40-goal scorers were Frank Mahovlich, Vic Hadfield, and Norm Ullman.

He had seen their contracts and I got the average, which was $75,000. He thought I'd screwed him, though I really wasn't trying to trick him.

I always found the negotiating to be a lot of fun though. In training camp we'd get a note in our cubicle. It would give a time for the appointment. Most of the time you went, Ivan would talk about everything but the contract. He had a funny accent and a nasal voice which made him difficult to understand at times.

For example, I remember a time when he talked about how his wife Dorothy had just spent $1,500 on grapes. Here I was, sitting in his office waiting for him to discuss my contract and all he wanted to talk about was this huge sum of money his wife had spent on grapes. I was baffled and couldn't figure what the hell he was on about.

During practice I skated up to Kenny Wharram, who had also had a contract negotiation that day.

"Kenny, does Tommy make wine or something?"

"What do you mean?"

"Well, he told me his wife Dorothy just spent $1,500 on grapes."

"He told me the same story," Kenny said, "but he said 'drapes,' not 'grapes.'"

During the summer of 1972, almost all the players were drafted by one of the WHA franchises. After draft day, everyone checked to see who they'd been drafted by. I was picked by the Miami Screaming Eagles. After the draft the other players always made terrible bird noises when I went out on the ice during practices.

Bordeleau was drafted by the Los Angeles Sharks. J.P. was certainly a bit gullible, so I told him that not only was the team called the Sharks, but they were going to have a fin mounted on the back of their uniform.

He thought about it for a few seconds and looked very serious.

"Do you think that will bother my deking?"

It became clear that summer that Bobby was thinking about joining the new league, and a few players had actually signed up before training camp started. What bothered Bobby was that players would get drafted by the WHA, get a contract offer, and then would come back to the NHL to use the offer to negotiate a higher deal. Bobby hated the guys whom he felt were using the WHA. Bobby felt the WHA was simply trying to help the players and that using the offers was pretty underhanded. These guys were never intending to leave, he said, and it made him angry.

A few months before he signed, we talked about the new league.

"If someone offered me $1 million, I'd go," he told me privately. "These guys who are approaching the WHA and then taking the contracts back to the NHL are blackmailing the owners."

Eventually he told the papers the same thing, never figuring that the WHA could get that kind of money together. A week later, he had the offer. The WHA had pooled their money to get Bobby to go to Winnipeg. He signed the contract soon after.

Billy Wirtz is a bullheaded guy. It's my opinion that he didn't think the WHA could make it. I don't think the WHA would have made it if Bobby hadn't gone. He was the flame that led other players to the league. Other notable stars, like Derek Sanderson, didn't make the move until Bobby had joined the new league.

The players on the Blackhawks all lobbied management to make an effort to keep Bobby, because we'd just gone to the seventh game of the Stanley Cup the year before and we thought with him we could eventually win a number of Cups. The players even said they'd give up a little bit of their salary so they could pay Bobby the extra amount.

I had decided I couldn't go unless Billy Reay also made the switch. My linemates would have had to go as well, so I stayed in Chicago. To this day, Billy Wirtz says Bobby cost the NHL a billion dollars in salaries. But even for me, the fact Bobby left created a huge jump in salaries.

At the start of the 1972–73 season, Bobby's departure led the Blackhawks management to become concerned that other stars were going to make the jump to the WHA now that Bobby had made the league respectable. Stan Mikita was hurt with a back injury, and with Bobby in Winnipeg, Martin, Pappin, and I were the team's main offence.

The three of us heard, soon after the season began, that we were going to be signed to long-term contracts which would last until we were 40. I was 30 at the time, so it was a 10-year contract. Pit was two years older, so they were going to sign him for eight years, and Jimmy was four years older, so he was going to be on contract for six.

I didn't have an agent and did all my own negotiations. I was making $75,000 at the time and figured that over ten years, $1 million would be fair. I thought I'd be set for life.

Billy Wirtz had told us that if we started the season, he would renegotiate longer deals. The contract negotiation came following a game in L.A. which we won 5–3. The MPH line had four of the goals in the game. After the next practice I got the note and went into see Tommy Ivan.

Without letting me get a thing in, he started at me.

"This is the most ridiculous thing I have ever heard of," Ivan said. "This is not my idea and you know I hate this thing. But I've been authorized to give you a one-time only offer. There are no negotiations here. This is the offer and you take it or leave it. For 10 years, we're prepared to give you $1.5 million."

I thought that maybe I had underestimated what was really going on. I hadn't even said a word and I was already half a million dollars ahead of what I thought I was going to be offered.

"No, I don't think I can do that," I told Ivan. "I was thinking of $1,750,000."

I should have come back with a figure of two million, but I wasn't sure what Ivan would do in response.

"It's out of the question," Ivan said, angrily picking up the phone. He dialed Billy Wirtz.

"Hull is being ridiculous, Mr. Wirtz. You're going to have to come over here. I told you this wasn't going to work."

Eventually Wirtz came over. We had built up a good relationship over the years and I must admit I thought he was a good owner.

"Relax, Tommy," Wirtz said. "Dennis, are you a gambler?"

"No," I replied, a little surprised by the question.

"Don't you go to the track or anything?" he said.

"No."

"Well, Dennis, how about I flip you for the extra $250,000?"

Well, I figured I was already a half a million ahead of where I thought I was going to be, so what was there to lose?

"Okay," I said.

He got a quarter out and flipped it.

"Call it!"

"Heads."

"It's heads," he said, looking at the coin. But I never saw it. Every time I see him now, I ask him about it.

"Billy, was it really heads?"

"Of course it was heads," he says, "do you think I give my money away?"

FOURTEEN

The Russians Are Coming

*B*ut Bobby leaving for the WHA wasn't the only turmoil the NHL saw in the summer of 1972. It was during that summer, almost at the last possible moment, that the NHL set up the Summit Series, a showdown between the Soviet national team and 40 NHL all-stars.

When the coaches for the team picked the players, I was really excited because Bobby and I were both chosen. The NHL protested and managed to get the WHA players excluded from the team.

The NHL owners said if any WHA player went to the series, then they wouldn't let their players go. There was talk that Prime Minister Pierre Trudeau was going to try to force the league to take players like Bobby, but I think the owners would have called off the series if it had come to that.

Because Bobby wasn't going to be allowed on the team, I told John Ferguson, one of the coaches, that I wouldn't go. He said he understood.

As August began, I was running a hockey school in Chicago and got the chance to talk to Bobby.

Bobby had been to Europe with a team in 1960. It was a combination of Rangers and Bruins, and they asked a few other players to come along. The team played 21 games in 25 nights and Bobby said that series taught him to pace himself.

"The Russians have been looking at this for a long time," he said. "And this is going to be a big thing, for professionals from North America to play the Russians. This is going to be a *big* deal. I already made my deal with Winnipeg, but why don't you go and represent us?"

I didn't argue with him and called Ferguson back. I didn't think he'd want me on the team, but he said my spot was still open. However, Bobby was upset nonetheless about not going to the series and still says it's the biggest disappointment in his hockey career.

The Canadian team faced a lot of obstacles from the start, though we didn't know it. Most guys took the summer off and had a good time. Training camp was for getting into shape. My first training camp was six weeks, which was a long grind. Current NHL squads play games three days after camp opens. The team also had nobody to play against, so there were only a few intra-squad games to get us warmed up.

I was excited to be playing with a team full of stars like Bobby Clarke and Jean Ratelle. Training camp was fun, not work, and guys who were running hockey schools would regularly leave for a day. No one thought it would be a big deal.

There were also a lot of players on the team — when the team lined up for a skating drill, there were eight left wingers.

The players also knew next to nothing about the Russians. Except for Gerry Pinder, a winger with the Blackhawks, who had played the Russians in Junior, I didn't know anyone who'd played against them.

"I know you guys are better than the Canadian National team," he said, "but these guys are really good."

We were overconfident. NHL scouts had been over to watch the Russian team and they said they weren't any good. Vladislav Tretiak had a bad game when the scouts were over and they came back saying that he wasn't much of a goaltender. There was also the rumour that the Russians set it up so that we'd believe it would be easy.

Everybody certainly wanted to play, but we thought it was going to be easy, and besides, we got a free trip to Europe and would get to play in Sweden. Hockey was almost incidental. The first game of the series was held in Montreal. We got the first two goals quickly and talk went around the bench that this was going to be almost too easy. It was going to be a cakewalk. And then we lost 7–3.

It was the biggest shock I ever had in hockey. There was panic on the team. We'd completely underestimated the Russians. I realized right off that their individual skills were better than most of the NHL players. They could flip the puck in the air the way most NHL players do now, but at the time, no one could do that. On an icing, they'd just flip it to the linesman. I'd never seen anyone do that before.

Their plays worked like clockwork, while we'd been practising ad hoc plays. The Russians had precise, intricate, weaving plays. It was also clear they were physically strong. I later found out it was because they'd done a lot of weight lifting, something that hadn't yet come into vogue in the NHL. All we'd done in training camp was a few sit-ups in the hall in Maple Leaf Gardens and all I remember about it was that we all laughed at Harry Sinden, the team's head coach, because he had a brown stain in the back of his underwear. It seemed like a joke to be doing exercise. Nobody had ever done anything to keep in shape during the off-season — all we did was play.

Without even playing against them, I knew the Russians were special. I thought Alex Yakushev and Valeri Kharlamov were outstanding. If they'd played in the NHL and played our style, there was no way we would have beaten them.

Their style dictated that they had to pass until they were right on top of the net. Yakushev could shoot harder than I could, but he'd be 15 feet out and still passing the puck rather than shooting. It didn't make sense. They'd score goals, but they only had 14 shots on net half the time, and their defencemen never shot from the point. This finally changed during the last game in Moscow when they started shooting from the point, but by then it was too late.

We realized the Russians were in condition to play like it was the Stanley Cup and we were in the condition to play in training camp. And there was a big gap between the two. The only person on the team who didn't panic was Harry Sinden.

By the end of the first game I understood that the team had to get into some sort of shape, but there wasn't time because we had to play and win our next game in Toronto.

We did manage to take that game 4–1, partly because I think the Russians had some of the overconfidence that was our problem in the first game. They thought the series was theirs.

It was after the second game that I began to notice the differences in cultures between the Canadian and Soviet players. In order to keep the players in line, the Soviet team had been told that the Canadian players were set up to look like they had everything they wanted. The Canadian players all had cars and, after the game, would get into their big seventies' style automobiles and drive home. The Russians were told the cars didn't belong to the players, that the cars were simply lent to the Canadian players to make the Russians look bad.

Their equipment was archaic. Their skates were castoffs from other teams. They sharpened their skates with stones. After that series the CCCP began supplying them with better equipment, but the team's equipment for the Summit Series wasn't even second rate. When we exchanged sweaters with them I couldn't believe how their jerseys smelled. It appeared they never washed them and it didn't bother them. It was really a different culture.

When we went to Winnipeg for game three, the team officials told me I was going to play, but when I got to the arena, Sinden told me he'd changed his mind. I was pretty disappointed, because I wanted to get on the ice where Bobby was going to play in the WHA. The game ended up tied 4–4. Though I didn't play in the first three games, I wasn't crushed by sitting. After all, there were forty players on the team and some of the players — like Mahovlich, Cashman, and Hadfield — had had tremendous seasons the year before. Richard Martin had just scored 50 goals and he wasn't playing, so I wasn't complaining.

The game in Vancouver was the first matchup where I saw action. I was a little anxious about playing because the one thing you don't want to do when you're the new guy in the lineup is to be the guy who caused the team to lose. When you're with a different group of guys, the confidence you have in one another isn't the same as the confidence I had when playing with the Blackhawks.

The Soviets, on the other hand, had been teammates for years. The Canadian team had been together for weeks. It's hard to become a team and figure out how guys think in less than a month. In Chicago I'd played with the same guys for quite a while. I knew their families and kids, and how they reacted and felt in any situation.

This new reality was brought home to me in training camp. In an intra-squad game, Harry sent me out to kill a penalty. I went out and Bobby Clarke was centring the line so I asked him where he wanted me to set up.

"On the bench," was the reply.

It was funny, but it emphasized how important it was to know the players around you.

It also made me nervous. My game was skating up and down the ice and blasting the puck, but I wasn't going to be able to do that against the Russians. And I hadn't played against anyone since the Rangers in the Stanley Cup the previous spring.

Jean Ratelle and Rod Gilbert were my linemates for the series. Ratelle was one of the nicest people I met in my career in the NHL.

"Don't think you have to do something special, Dennis," he said as we were getting ready to hit the ice. "Just play your own game and do your job. Don't do more than you can do."

As soon as he said this, I began to feel better and followed his advice.

I scored the third goal, but we lost the game 5–3. My goal against the Russians did teach me something important about the way they thought. They worked as hard stopping that third goal as they had the first, even though they were up by four. I knew then that they weren't going to just roll over and give up.

In Vancouver, following the game, the fans booed us off the ice. That's when Phil Esposito, who became a superstar following his departure from Chicago, grabbed a microphone and yelled at the fans, telling them that we'd given up our summer, were doing the best we can, and that the players deserved more than this.

The funny thing about Phil is that he knew he was going to do well in the series. Before the first game in Montreal, we went out for dinner and had a discussion about how the series was going to go.

"I usually average a couple of points a game," he said, "so I should end up with 15 or 16 points in the series."

Of course, he did.

After the loss in Vancouver, the players drew together and came closer as a team. We headed to Stockholm to play the Swedish national team, which turned out to be our saving grace.

FIFTEEN

Moses Walks Among Us

*T*he Blackhawks had five players among the forty on the team. Along with me, Pat Stapleton, Tony Esposito, Bill White, and Stan Mikita went. The Chicago management wouldn't let us all fly on the same plane when we took the flight to Stockholm. If something happened they didn't want to lose all their key players at once. Because of their concern, when we went to Europe, White, Stapleton, and Mikita went on one plane and I travelled with Tony.

When we got back I talked to Tommy Ivan about the set-up for the flights.

"Tommy, there's something that's been bothering me."

"Yeah, what is it," he said gruffly.

"If a plane was going to crash, which one did you want to go down?"

He looked at me strangely, but never really did come up with an answer.

The two games we played in Stockholm proved to be invaluable in the long run. The more the team played together, the closer we became. We got more comfortable with each other as players and as people. We were getting used to the bigger ice surface and making jokes about needing a transfer if you went off your wing.

Sweden had a good team, but we were getting fired up.

The team also had a lot of fun in Stockholm. We played the Swedish national team twice and won 4–1 and tied 4–4. I got a couple of goals, though I doubt anyone kept track. The best thing about playing in Sweden was the advertisements they projected on the ice between periods. The lights would go down and these ads would show up. Most of them were for porn shops — stuff that would never be shown at a game in North America.

Things weren't looking good for us when we arrived and even the Canadian ambassador to Sweden took time out to rip a shred off us in the paper. We were told we were dirty players, but we were just trying to keep up with the European style of play. The Swedish team played like the Russians. They kicked and speared — things we weren't used to — and we reacted. The ambassador said we were thugs. When we went to the embassy for a reception, Phil Esposito gave her a hard time.

"What's wrong with you?" he asked. "You don't even have any Canadian beer." Nationalism had sunk in. We would drink the local Swedish beer when we were out on the town, but Phil thought there should be Canadian beer.

"You can't get it here," she said.

"Why not? There's a flight in here everyday!"

One of the main characters on the team was Wayne Cashman. Cashman lived hard. He'd party all night and he'd hit the ice and still be the best player. I was amazed. I had seen Mikita and Esposito, but this guy was a wildman and he'd still be the best player the next day. We used to play guilty — Bobby used to say he played best when he was playing guilty for what he'd done the night before — but nothing like Cash. Wayne never actually played in Moscow because of what had happened in Sweden. The problem was that Cash embraced the European style of play and became known as the "Butcher of Barcelona." He could spear and slash anyone. Ulf Sterner, who had played briefly in the mid-sixties with the Rangers, took a run at Cash during the first game. Cash went to spear him and Ulf raised his stick and hit

Cash right in the mouth, splitting his tongue down the middle.

I watched them sew his tongue up while he sat on the bench. It had to be incredibly painful. The trainer put 40 stitches in his tongue, which had swollen up and looked like a tennis ball. It was pretty clear that Cash wasn't going to be back for the rest of the games against Russia. Following the game Dale Tallon and I went out for a beer with Bobby Orr, who had injured his knee before the series but travelled with the team. We went to a bar called Chat Noir and just after we sat down, Cash came walking in and motioned to the bartender for a beer and a straw. He sat down at our table tried to talk to me. But his tongue was so swollen that he couldn't speak sensibly and I couldn't understand him. Eventually it wore me out.

"Cash, just write it down."

So he took a beer coaster and wrote: "I always wanted to speak French."

Finally, two weeks after the game in Vancouver, the team flew into Moscow. Moscow was a unique and amazing city. I remember being struck by the number of people lined up at bus stops. There seemed to be hundreds of people waiting for buses. There were also very few cars. Gorky Blvd., which had six lanes, seemed to only have four or five cars on it at rush hour. It wasn't like any North American city — the whole atmosphere was foreign to me.

Soon after we arrived in Moscow, I was approached by a reporter asking what I thought of the city. I told him it looked a lot like Buffalo and, truthfully, it did. I didn't mean it to be a slam, it just looked like Buffalo to me. But the papers in North America gave the quote a lot of play. When I got back and played in Buffalo there were all types of banners saying, "Hull — go back to Moscow." But I hadn't meant it to be derogatory. Moscow was a nice city — the people in Buffalo should have thought I was saying their city was world class.

I wasn't the only one who found Russia to be a mystifying place. Sue had come on the trip and it was clear she was going to have some trouble adapting to Russia. After the first practice, I went to the hotel.

"How was lunch?"

"I'm never eating there again," she said.

"Why not?"

"Because my soup looked back at me."

Apparently she'd had soup with fish eyes in it and for the rest of the trip, I had to check her food before she'd eat it.

Soon after we arrived, Canadian players began to complain about getting calls in the middle of the night. To this day, Phil Esposito thinks the calls were placed by Russian officials who were trying to scare us. I don't think that's the case, though. It was Canadians who made the calls. There were a lot of fans who travelled with the team to watch the games and were staying in the same hotel.

My father-in-law was there, but he was on a different floor. To call my room, he had to dial 13 numbers. There were certainly lots of mistakes. Phil might have believed the Russians were out to toy with our minds, but I didn't believe it for a minute.

The Russian fans loved us. Many of them had read the *Hockey News* in Russian and knew all the players. We'd also come prepared for the kids who congregated around our every move. We had packages of bubble gum ready.

The problem was that the Russian soldiers had been told to surround the bus and not let anyone near it. They had guns and seemed to be ready to use them. When we went to give the gum to the kids, the Russian troops weren't very happy, and yelled at us to stop.

But we gave the gum to the kids anyway, throwing it out into the crowd. A package of gum landed at the feet of one of the soldiers. A kid went to reach for it and the soldier stepped on the kid's hand. That infuriated Brad Park and Bill White, and the two went over to confront the soldier.

It quickly became apparent that he'd never had any sort of confrontation before. A Russian soldier rarely gets an argument. This soldier simply expected people to obey him. But when Brad and Bill questioned him, he didn't know what to do and just turned around and walked away.

Stapleton was also at his best while we were in Moscow. He pulled a couple of stunts, including an occasion when he got ten guys on a bus by telling them he was taking them to the Moscow Golf and Country Club. Another time he told the same guys that he was taking them out for Chinese food.

I wanted to see Moscow, so Pat and I got a tour of Red Square. The tour guide was a young Russian girl and one of the highlights of the tour was seeing Lenin's tomb.

Pat approached her and said he was looking for some information.

"Hey, can you tell me how long Stalin has been in there anyway?"

I thought the girl was going to freak out.

"It's Mr. Lenin!"

"Are you sure?" Pat said. "I thought it was Stalin. Isn't he the nice guy?"

*B*efore the fifth game, Vic Hadfield, Richard Martin, Gilles Perrault, and Jocelyn Guevremont left the team and went home. Though some have criticized them for leaving, I didn't really blame them. By the time we got to Moscow, the team was set. It was clear that they weren't going to play and they were frustrated by it, so they went back to their training camps, which were up and running. Hadfield and Martin were both left wingers, so it opened up the possibility that I would get some ice time.

It was funny though, because the guys who were left were certainly not the best known. It was J.P. Parise, Dennis Hull, and Paul Henderson — not exactly household names. But we were the ones who ended up playing. Harry wanted a team. It wasn't a collection of stars, but a team. And the more we played together, the closer we got. There were a lot of guys on the periphery. We knew the guys who sat out were good, but they didn't fit in with Harry's idea of the team.

We opened a big lead in the fifth game, but dropped it 5–4 after a terrible third period. It was during that game, though, that Paul Henderson started to shine.

Henderson wasn't a born-again Christian at the time, and he certainly liked to go out and have a good time. He wasn't as bad as Cash — no one really could have been — but he liked to have fun.

Henderson certainly was not a star. If he hadn't scored the goals during that series, he probably wouldn't even be remembered. He was pretty ordinary before that and pretty ordinary after that. But for 28 days in September, he was unbelievable. Maybe he's right when he says he was placed on this earth to score those goals in the Summit Series.

It certainly would have been different had Cashman scored the goals. Because he was a great skater, the big ice surface suited his game. He wasn't a great stick handler, but he could skate with anyone in the NHL.

Before I took the ice in game six, Paul approached me.

"Dennis, you're the new guy, so you've got to be our Moses and lead us," he said.

Well, it was Paul, not me, who turned out to be our Moses.

SIXTEEN

Divine Intervention

I had read about communism, but it wasn't until I got to Russia that I saw how it worked. After one of our first practices, my wife and I went for a walk through Red Square, which was stunning. We saw a lot of newly wed Russian couples getting their pictures taken in Red Square. As we were walking around the walls of the Kremlin, an army jeep pulled up. An army officer jumped out of the jeep, took 20 shovels out of the back and leaned them against a bench. He then proceeded to point at people in the crowd, who walked over to him without argument. Most took off their jackets and grabbed a shovel, walked to the nearby garden and starting working. They turned the garden over, and once they finished the job, they grabbed their coats and continued on their way.

Sue turned to me and said, "This is communism." I was amazed. I was commenting on how exceptional it was to even see this when my wife pointed out my camera was still around my neck. I had never taken a picture.

Another time I noticed a soft drink machine up against a wall which contained the hot flavour in Russia at the time, which was plum. It wasn't like a conventional North American pop machine, though. If you wanted a drink, you would place money into it and lift a glass that was on a chain. The machine would fill up the glass and you'd drink and put the glass back and the next person would use it. No paper, no cans. Nothing disposable. The stores were also unusual. There were shelves full of goods, but shoes could be next to fish. There didn't appear to be any order. You had to line up to get into the store. I watched a man buy shoes while I was there. The shoes were all the same —black, made of leather. The only difference was size. He'd find the size and get in a line-up to get the shoes and then line up to pay. It seemed like endless line-ups. It was very strange.

Because of the peculiarities of Russian consumer goods, we were even told to bring our own toilet paper. Russian toilet paper was terrible stuff. (A few years ago at a banquet I was introducing Dick Butkus, the Chicago linebacker. "Dick Butkus is like Russian toilet paper," I told the crowd. "He's rough and tough and doesn't take shit from anybody.")

Perhaps some of the culture shock came from the fact that most of the Russian players couldn't speak any English. At least that was the case with Evgeny Zimin, the guy I played against in the last four games.

We played line to line and he never said a word to me. And because I thought he didn't speak English, I never attempted to talk to him.

At the end of the series I was waiting by the dressing room and someone came up to me, but I wasn't paying much attention.

"Dennis, can I have your stick?" he said in clear English.

I started looking around before I realized it was Zimin who was talking to me.

*E*ven though we were down by two games, the team had begun clicking and we knew we could win. In the sixth game, I scored in the second period and Henderson put in the winner as we took the game 3–2. It was also the first game in which we began having problems with the German referee, who called bizarre penalties against the Canadian team. Both Henderson's play and the strange officiating stayed constant for the rest of the series.

At the start of the sixth game, we gave the Russians these beautiful Stetson hats. As I went by the Russian dressing room afterwards, they were all in the garbage. They weren't allowed to keep them, which goes a long way in demonstrating just how much the coaches and politicians controlled their players.

I found it hard to adjust to the Russian style of play. They played a different style, and had a different style of aggression. Our defencemen would regularly have to change the laces on their skates because they'd be cut when the Russians would kick at them.

I got a penalty in game six when I was playing against Yakushev. I was skating alongside him when all of a sudden, he looked over at me and spat in my face. I turned and smashed him with my stick, because it had never happened to me before. It was just my reaction, and despite the fact the media was making us out to be bullies, many of the penalties were a reaction to a style of play we weren't familiar with.

The Russians didn't chase pucks into the corners. If you don't follow the puck into the corners, then you don't last long in the NHL. It's probably a stupid thing to head into the corners and get smashed by a body-check, but it's part of our game. The Russians wouldn't do it. They'd stop and let the Canadian player go into the corner and then they'd try to take the puck from him. People thought it was because they were afraid, but it was just part of their game.

Despite the disparity in the styles of play between the two teams, Pat had the Russians' system figured out by the time I started playing. I, on the other hand, could be still playing the Russians thirty years later and not have their passing patterns figured out.

It's like Billy used to say: "Give it to Dennis in front of the net and watch him panic."

*H*enderson and Phil led us to a 4–3 win in the seventh game, meaning the series would be decided by the final game. Tony's play in that game was so amazing that the Russians asked if they could run tests on him. They couldn't figure out how a pudgy, seemingly out-of-shape goaltender could play as well as he had. They came to the conclusion that his heart was bigger than anyone else's. I could have told them that, and he wouldn't have had to take any test. Dryden was our other goalie during the series, and in many ways, he seemed more normal than any goaltender I'd played with before. The only strange thing about Dryden was you needed a thesaurus to figure out what he was talking about. The one thing about players and goalies is that there isn't much of a connection. It's a different sport. A goalie gets shot at. Guys who play have no idea how they do it or why they'd want to do it. They're different.

For example, Tony wouldn't let anyone talk to him on game day and Glenn was always throwing up, so I suppose anyone would have seemed normal. Gary Smith, whom the Blackhawks received in a trade in 1971 from California, would go to the dressing room between periods and take off all his equipment and take a shower.

"Smitty, are you hurt?" Reay asked him the first time he went through his routine.

"No Billy, I do this in every game."

Removing his equipment distracted him so he wouldn't have to think about the actual game — he had it timed so it took the full 15 minutes.

*D*espite the fact Sue was never a hockey fan, she did go to most of the games in Moscow. But she found the Canadian fans, who had travelled with the team to Russia, to be crude, and decided she didn't want to go to the last game; she stayed in the hotel to watch it on the television. Gary Bergman's wife also stayed in the hotel, so the two of them gathered around a TV to watch the final.

In the middle of the game, Bergman got speared in front of the net. Mrs. Bergman, obviously annoyed by this, shouted at the television, "Kick him in the bag!"

Sue said it was as bad as being at the game.

*H*enderson's goal in the final game has had an amazing impact on hockey. But to me, the most amazing fact is that Tretiak didn't stop it. Any North American goalie would have left his crease and knocked the puck aside, but Tretiak stayed put. He just stood there as Henderson knocked it by him.

In many ways, Tretiak didn't play the same way as Dryden or Esposito. He didn't cut the angles off. He stayed in his net. The thing that I think about is that, years later, when he was 33 or 34, he had a chance to come to the NHL and didn't do it. Everyone else wanted to come, so why would this premier goalie not come and try his luck? Did he know his style wouldn't suit the NHL? I don't know. I had dinner with him recently at Mahovlich's place and I asked him why he didn't give it a try.

"Oh, I was too old," he said.

"God, Johnny Bower was 40 years old when he played — you could have done it."

But he wouldn't give me a definitive answer. I think he knew his style wasn't going to work. I like to kid him about the goal whenever I see him.

"Hey Vladdy, that goal made you famous. If you'd stopped it, you'd be driving a cab in Moscow right now."

SEVENTEEN

Czech Mate

I went to Phil Esposito's room after the game to celebrate and was there until the early morning. The thing most people don't know about the Summit Series is that the eighth game in Moscow wasn't the last game we played. The morning following the win, we had to head to Czechoslovakia to play the national team. The Czechs were the World Champions from the previous year, meaning the game wasn't going to be easy.

In a strange twist of fate, the referee for the game in Prague was Kompalla, the official Parise had threatened to kill in the final game. In fact, Kompalla was on the same flight as the Canadian national team. Although we knew Kompalla had been told what to do by the Russian officials, J.P. still hated him. Kompalla was terrified about what J.P. might do him. For the entire flight, Kompalla just sat in his seat looking worried and shaking slightly.

Just as they served dinner, J.P. approached him. I think Kompalla thought he was going to be beaten, but J.P. just tipped the referee's dinner into his lap. Kompalla sat there and didn't move a muscle in protest.

Following the previous night's festivities, not many of the players were in playing condition. While we were in the airport after landing in Czechoslovakia, Harry picked the team that would play.

"Everybody up against the wall," he said as we were getting off the flight. He lined everyone up and looked at each player.

"You look like you can play," he'd say to one player. "You don't look in very good shape," to another. Despite being up for almost the entire night before the early morning flight, I was picked.

In Prague, we could walk from our hotel to the rink, and before the game this tall man came up to me.

"Are you with Team Canada?" he said. It was apparent he was Czechoslovakian.

"Sure am," I replied.

"Well, what's it like in the NHL?" he asked, the first of several questions he fired my way.

I talked to this fellow for a few minutes and eventually I asked him whether this was one of the streets the Russian tanks had come down to stop the revolution in 1968.

"How did you know that?" he said.

"The whole world knows that!"

But he didn't believe anyone outside of Czechoslovakia knew about what had happened. Finally the conversation wore down and I walked into the arena.

I got changed and went out on the ice to warm up. Just as Kompalla was getting ready to drop the puck, I looked at the centerman for the Czech team — he was the guy who'd had the conversation with me, Vaclav Nedomansky. After the opening face off, he took the puck, skated around the defence and scored. Ned, as I now call him, would become a good friend.

In 1974 he escaped from Czechoslovakia. The officials knew he was a flight risk, so they took his passport away. But he had two of them, a personal one and a passport for the team. He lived in the north part of Czechoslovakia and he was aware that his house was bugged. He and his wife had most of their conversations about escaping in the bathroom and they'd leave the water running.

One day, he went and got his son from school and drove south as far as he could. Eventually he crossed into Austria, and kept driving until his car ran out of gas. He was still afraid the Czech officials would find his family.

In 1978, when I was playing with Detroit, we played the Czech national team. The players on the team said the Czech officials had closed the borders from the north to the south so that Nedomansky couldn't leave. He got through about 15 minutes before they closed the southern crossing.

When he played in Detroit, he rented Pit Martin's house in Windsor. Martin had bought the house from a dentist who had gone bankrupt and it had all the luxuries of a mansion. After the game, Nedomansky took a few of the players from the Czech team to his house. When they saw the place, they were amazed.

"Ned, is this your house?" one of the amazed Czech players asked.

"No, are you kidding?" he said. "This is just a 20-goal-scorer's house."

Stan Mikita had gone to Czechoslovakia ahead of the team, partly because he hadn't been playing and partly because the Czech game was a homecoming for him. Stan was Czechoslovakian by birth and his mother had shuttled him out of the country when he was a young boy, so his mother had never seen him play. In 1945, when the Russians were coming into Czechoslovakia, Stan's mother sent him to St. Catharines with his sister. Stan was 13 at the time and didn't speak English. He lived with his aunt and uncle, whom he referred to as his mother and father.

He was in a bar in Prague watching the eighth game when a loud Russian started shooting his mouth off about how the Soviet team was going to beat the Canadians.

"If the Russians win, I'll buy everyone in this bar a beer," the Russian said.

"Well, if the Canadians win," Stan said, "you should buy everyone champagne."

"OK," he agreed.

Of course, when the Canadians won, the Russian reneged on the deal and wouldn't pay. The game we played in Prague was an amazing experience for Stan. In Czechoslovakia, he was a national hero.

I think, like seeing Bobby's number retired in Winnipeg, it was one of the most moving experiences of my life. When Stan, who was my captain with the Blackhawks, was introduced, the sellout crowd clapped and cheered for ten minutes. I had tears streaming down my face, especially when they brought his mother down onto the ice.

When we flew out of Prague, the NHL said we had to have two planes, but the players said there was no way we were going back on two planes. Because of our protests, Air Canada sent a 707 for the 40 players and personnel. It was loaded with food and alcohol. While we were in Prague, we were taken to crystal stores and given crystal glasses. Cashman and Peter Mahovlich had brandy snifters and they poured an entire bottle of whiskey into these glasses. Then the two started toasting one another. I turned to Bill White and told him there was no way the two glasses would ever make it back to Canada. Sure enough, about half way through the flight there was the crashing sound of glass hitting the floor.

When the plane landed, we had been told we were going to be met by Prime Minister Pierre Trudeau. Dr. Bull, the team doctor, was the biggest Trudeau fan ever and had spent the last couple of days of our trip looking forward to the meeting. But he fell asleep on the plane. Pat Stapleton got a scalpel out of the doctor's bag and cut all the stitches in the doctor's sleeve except for one or two that remained to hold it on.

When we got out of the plane, Pat followed the doctor to the meeting with Trudeau.

"Mr. Trudeau, it's a pleasure to meet you," the doctor said.

At that moment, Stapleton pulled his sleeve and it came right off and rolled down his arm. Trudeau actually thought the incident was rather funny.

Pranks were par for the course that day.

John Ferguson, the assistant coach on the team, had spent much of the trip getting a stick autographed by everyone involved in the series. It was his pride and joy. Serge Savard hung around until Ferguson went to shake the Prime Minister's hand. Savard walked up, took the stick out of Ferguson's hands, and handed it to Trudeau.

"Here, Mr. Prime Minister," he said, "this is for you."

There was nothing Ferguson could do. After all, it was the Prime Minister. A day or two later, Trudeau heard about the stunt and gave the stick back.

Trudeau knew everything about the series, and it was clear that he had watched it closely. But Eagleson, who was a dyed-in-the-wool Conservative through and through, wanted to make the whole affair very political. He was concerned about what door we went out following the flight. The whole thing had been set up so the Prime Minister would meet us at a certain spot at the airport and Eagleson wanted to screw up those plans. It said a lot about him: we'd just won the series of the century and he was worried about embarrassomg the prime minister.

For the trip, each player was given luggage, and on the luggage was a red sticker with your number on it. I was #10 and Bobby Clarke was #16. When we were riding around in the fire truck with the Prime Minister, I got one of my stickers out and began talking with Trudeau.

"What did you think of the series, Mr. Prime Minister?" I said, slapping him on the back with the sticker so it stuck to his coat. Not to be outdone, Clarke followed suit. "So how about that goal by Esposito?" Bobby said to Trudeau, slapping a number 10 on the back of the PM's suit.

So there we were, bombing through this parade in Montreal and the Prime Minister has the numbers "10" and "16" on the back of his suit. I'm sure someone in the parade saw it and wondered why — well, now you know.

I'm still amazed about the whole experience. When I started working as a speaker at banquets in late 1977, I used to preface my account of the series by saying that everyone over five years old knew where they were when Henderson scored. Now it's everyone over 30. It's a remarkable phenomenon. There have been some great series since and hockey has come a long way, but none of the international series since 1972 hold the same prestige.

I've attended the series' reunions and they've been special, and the Russian players attended the fifth, tenth, and twentieth anniversaries, though they couldn't come over for the twenty-fifth anniversary gathering. For the twentieth anniversary, we played reunion games against the Russians in Hamilton, Saskatoon, Vancouver, and Ottawa. The Russians were still under communism and there were security officers who looked like they might be KGB travelling with the team. I guess these officials had told the Russian players to be more like the Canadians and drink beer, not vodka, when they were in Canada.

That didn't sit well with Bill White, who was very fond of the Russian players. When we got watches for the reunion, Bill was in tears because the Russians hadn't received the gift as well. The sentiment ran deep on the Canadian team. Following the series and the reunions, we knew most of the Russians as well as we knew our teammates on Team Canada in Ottawa, there was a bar in the Civic Centre at Frank Clair Stadium. Though the Russians were only supposed to drink beer, White managed to get a number of bottles of vodka. He kept them under the counter and, as he was the bartender at one of our post-game gatherings, he poured vodka for the Russian players whenever they came over for beer.

After a couple of hours of this, we had to leave. We had to carry the Russian players out, which annoyed their officials greatly.

"What happened?" one asked. "You were supposed to behave like the Canadians!"

The most interesting part of the reunion for the Russians was the hotel televisions. They had access to the pay-per-view programs and, needless to say, some of the programs were rather explicit. The Russians had never seen anything like them before. They couldn't believe that showing this kind of stuff was legal, but it was all they wanted to watch. Around the same time, Henderson gave each of the Soviet players a bible translated into Russian. Maybe the bibles cancelled out the dirty movies.

From Ottawa, we went over to Hull with Yakushev, a big tall guy and looks a lot like Eric Nesterenko. As we were heading over the bridge, Yakushev saw the sign "Hull," and asked the driver to stop the car in the middle of the bridge.

He got out of the car and looked at the sign.

"Son of a bitch," Yakushev said, and then he looked at me. "They name whole cities after you?"

Once we got to *my* city, the Russians wanted to go the topless bars, but they didn't have any money. Dale Tallon, one of the players on Team Canada who never saw any ice time, gave them his Visa card. Dale said when he got it back, the numbers were worn right off the plastic. While in the bar, the Russians tried hard to make up for lost opportunities.

"I'm taking you home," Vikto Kuzkin, the Russian defence-man, said to one of the dancers.

The funny thing was that she agreed and asked where "home" was.

"Moscow," was the reply.

That slowed her down.

It was amazing to see them again, but it's also sad to hear what's happened to some of them. The best job many can get is a cab driver in Moscow, because there's lots of foreign money in it.

In Saskatoon, there was a lunch put on with a big spread. In the middle of one of the trays, there was a pineapple, which was the cause of a great deal of murmuring among the Russian players. It turned out they'd never seen a pineapple. Though no one ever eats the pineapple at these things, the Russians insisted on taking it with them to their rooms. Eventually one of us had to go up and show them how to core the damned thing.

At the end of the reunion, the Soviet players wanted us to go over to Russia, but they couldn't pay our way over. When the Russians came here, they got their expenses paid and some money on top for making the trip. But there was no money to go over to the USSR; I wanted to go and was willing to pay my way, but no one seemed to want to do it.

All things change, but most of the guys are the same, just older. However a lot of the wives probably aren't old enough to remember the series in 1972. During the most recent reunion, in 1997, there was a private dinner at the Royal York Hotel in Toronto for the players, and Serge Savard pointed out the disparity.

"Hey Dennis, it's good to see all the guys again," he said to me during the dinner, then added, "Funny, it looks like a lot of them took a mulligan on their wives."

The Russians didn't make the most recent reunion. There wasn't enough money to pay for them to all come over and most of them couldn't pay their own way. But I did get to meet Prime Minister Jean Chrétien when he came to the Hockey Hall of Fame. He walked into the Hall, and with all of these great players scattered about, he walked right over to me. I'd only seen him on television and had never had the opportunity to meet him.

"You're a funny son of a bitch," were the first words he said to me. I was amazed. The Prime Minister actually knew who I was. There are 30 million people in this country and he knew who I was.

He proceeded to stand and talk hockey for half an hour. Then he gave a speech about how much the series had meant to Canada. Eventually he had to leave and walked straight across the room to tell me it had been nice talking with me. My wife said she'd never seen me that thrilled, but it was the Prime Minister, and he actually knew who I was!

At the centre of the reunion's festivities was a game we played in Maple Leaf Gardens. Though I hadn't played for five years, I did manage to score a goal and mentioned to Henderson that I hoped this one worked out for me as well as his goal had worked for him.

EIGHTEEN

A Deal Almost Sealed

A number of things had changed by the time I was back at training camp in the fall of 1972. Bobby had gone to the WHA, and I had just played in what would turn out to be the biggest hockey series in history. Billy Reay had said it was fine if the Chicago players went to play in the Summit Series, but argued that hockey would never be the same again. He believed we'd become too familiar with one another and some of the competitiveness would disappear.

He was right in a way. You got to know the players and understand how they thought. Then you'd find yourself re-evaluating them and finding out they were actually different people than you thought they were. It was really hard to be as competitive against them as you had been before.

Players began to change as well. Originally, when I started playing, my teammates would just have some soap and deodorant at the arena. Eventually, when Cliff Koroll and Keith Magnuson came to the team, there would start to be shampoo and conditioner around. Following that was hair spray and hair dryers. I remember the first time someone used a hair dryer. Billy ran into the dressing room to find out what all the noise was about.

These new beauty tools wreaked havoc with Billy, who was from the old school of hockey. After one practice Billy came off the ice wearing the white undershirt he regularly wore when he directed our drills. I guess he decided he needed to put on some deodorant, because he reached over and grabbed a can and sprayed it under his arms. Someone pointed it out to him that it was hair spray.

"What's this game coming to?" he said as he walked out of the dressing room with his arms out at his sides.

The team changed, too. With Bobby gone, the Blackhawks still had a reputation as a great team, but we were not quite as dangerous as we had been before. A lot of teams still lacked the confidence they needed to beat us, and for a year or two after Bobby was gone, that worked to our advantage.

When I started back with the Blackhawks, more importance was placed on my play. My rise was a matter of ice time. You can play with stats in a funny way, but after Bobby left I got to play more and had more chances where I could score, especially on the power-play.

Meanwhile, Bobby had a hard time in Winnipeg. He told me that one of the first times he pulled on the Winnipeg socks, he began to question himself about the move. Not only did he play, but he had to do public relations for the league. On the day of a game in Chicago, we'd just relax, but if Bobby went to Cincinnati, he had to do a seemingly endless series of interviews. He'd just get to the rink in time for the game and was always expected to be the star as well.

The new salaries brought changes too. There was a big change in the way the players saw the team. The management didn't have the same degree of control over the players. The ownership couldn't dominate us any more. The whole structure of the team changed as guys switched leagues and bounced from team to team. The Blackhawks were also drafting players, like Darcy Rota, and giving them $100,000 advances.

Billy approached me during one of the first training practices

Rota attended and it was clear he thought things were swinging too far the other way.

"This guy, Darcy Rota, is getting $100,000?" Billy questioned. "God, I hope he can do electrical work around here as well."

Players' salaries were escalating more than they ever had and it affected us. It was noticeable when we got Dick Redmond, who had 44 points the year he was traded to Chicago. He made more money than Pit or Jimmy or myself. Before the WHA, Bobby and Stan made more money because they were better players. But after the new league started up, players made more money if they were better negotiators. There was a resentment among some players as well.

I had no complaints after the deal I'd made with Chicago. The first practice after I signed my contract, Billy Reay approached me.

"It's great for you, Dennis," he said. "But now you've got to play to the level of that contract."

It did add some pressure to the game for me, but the team managed to get through the playoffs in 1973, and once more take on the Canadiens for the Stanley Cup. I netted 39 goals in 1972–73 and had 51 assists, which amounted to my best statistical year in the NHL.

The 1972–73 Stanley Cup wasn't as exciting as the previous ones had been for me. Henri Richard was finished and Montreal needed another star from Quebec to take his place. Sam Pollock, the Canadiens' general manager, could usually make deals with teams that were desperate. He wanted Guy Lafleur. When it didn't look like he could get him in the draft, he traded for Oakland and Los Angeles' first-round picks to ensure Montreal would get their native son.

It took Lafleur a while to get going, but he fit the mould that fans of the Canadiens liked. Though it was years before I worked as a teacher, Guy still claims it was I who taught him to speak English. The incident in question occurred in 1971. Lafleur was the latest star on the Canadiens, but I wasn't familiar with him. I used to know more about young players when they came up.

For example, I knew about Bobby Orr because I'd played Junior against him, but I didn't really know who Lafleur was because he'd played in Quebec. He developed into a good player, but I didn't think much of him when I first played against him.

During one game, Lafleur's stick came up and clipped me.

"Hey, don't do that," I said.

"Je ne parle pas anglais," was Lafleur's response.

In the second period he whacked me again and I was pretty angry this time.

"What the hell did you do that for?" I yelled.

"Je ne parle pas anglais."

In the third period he was backchecking and he got way ahead of me as I crossed the red line. There were two defencemen back for the Canadiens, so I had nowhere to go. Remembering what had happened, I decided I'd slap the puck Lafleur's way. I let the shot fly and it struck him right on the ass.

We went to the faceoff circle and he looked right at me.

"Guess I won't hit you with my stick any more," he said in perfect English.

I don't think he was on the same level as Bobby or Henri Richard, although he was a great player, playing in a town with a great tradition, something I always envied. I'd loved to have played in Canada, where hockey has such a history and it's the centre of attention. In Toronto, people were more aware of the players. In Chicago, people weren't as aware of the game and didn't know about the players the way the Toronto or Montreal fans did.

The Stanley Cup was interesting that year for another reason: The WHA was playing its initial finals at the same time we were playing the Canadiens. Bobby had led Winnipeg to the championship against Hartford. One of the games was played to a score of 7–6, which we thought was pretty funny. Obviously the WHA wasn't as good a league as the NHL if the two best teams could play to such a high score. The only thing was that the fifth game of the Stanley Cup ended with an even higher score. I scored the first goal on a shot from outside the blue line on Ken Dryden and assisted on a goal by Jimmy Pappin in the second. It went back and forth and finally we were up 8–7 late in the game and the Canadiens pulled Dryden. Jimmy got the puck in their end and passed it to me with the empty net looming, and then threw his stick away. That moment has become one of the most profound memories I have of my career in hockey. He knew if he passed it to me, I'd give it back so he threw his stick away. He wanted me to score. I was so shocked that Guy Lapointe managed to catch up with me and hook me from behind and I didn't even put the puck in the net. After the game, Billy came up to Stapleton.

"Pat, do you realize that you were on the ice tonight for 15 goals!"

We dropped the series to the Canadiens four games to two. Montreal had taken another one away from me.

The following seasons were strange. The Philadelphia Flyers became a dominant team the year after we lost to the Canadiens. Philadelphia was a scary place to play. They'd cry havoc and send out the dogs of war. There was also a gang mentality where they'd put all their tough guys out and attack. We had our tough guys, though. Guys like John Marks, Grant Mulvey, and Keith Magnuson could have been brawlers too, but Billy insisted they play rather than fight. Billy wanted the game to be played the way it should be played, but we had a measure of success because our guys wouldn't back down.

Dave Schultz was their bruiser. I understood what he was doing. It was the only way he could stay in the league. He once went to the coach and said he wasn't good enough to play in the league. The coach at the time, Fred Shero, told him to relax because he was getting a lot more room around the net. That's because players were afraid to get too close to him and so he began scoring a few goals.

But it was a team concept. All of the Flyers would jump in and fight against players who weren't interested in fighting. I wasn't a fighter, but I worried about players getting hurt. I never tangled with the Flyers. They also played a lot rougher at home than they did on the road, which suggests the team wasn't as tough as they were made out to be. They won the Stanley Cup, but once the team was broken up and the players started going in other directions, they didn't prove to be quite as tough.

They did have talent, though. Clarke, Bill Barber, and Reg Leach were excellent players. If they'd won a few more Stanley Cups, they might have changed hockey. But Montreal was a more talented team and took them down in 1976. Boston was another tough team and they beat us in the playoffs another year to keep us from going to the Stanley Cup final for a third straight year.

Meanwhile, the Blackhawks were changing the make-up of the team. There were new players, and though the old guys were all Billy's players, the new ones didn't fit in with Billy's thoughts on the game. It caused some friction. Some of the new guys would be off the ice as soon as practice was done. But that wasn't Billy's way. Most of us veterans would be on the ice for an hour after practice was officially over. It was a new breed of player. I'd always been a Chicago Blackhawk. These guys only became Blackhawks when they were drafted the previous June. I began to wonder how much longer I would be playing hockey.

A factor in my decision was a hit I had taken from Barclay Plager in the 1973–74 season. Plager always had luck against me — I think I was even hit by Plager once while getting on a bus. In this case, I was coming across centre ice and he hit me cleanly. I flipped over and landed in a sitting position. I couldn't feel my arms or legs. I was paralyzed for what seemed like 10 minutes.

Billy was on the bench and he saw what had happened. He later told me it was only seconds that I had been unable to move, but that didn't reassure me much. I had nightmares afterwards about being paralyzed about the feeling or lack of feeling. The experience was scary. Nothing seemed that important afterwards.

Maybe my spine was bruised for a second, but I had nightmares that it would happen again. It affected the way I played because I would think about it on the ice. When you add that to the changes going on in Chicago, I knew my career was near the end.

It wasn't my first encounter with Plager though. When I was playing a Junior game in Peterborough, I had my head down as I was bringing the puck up and, out of nowhere, Plager hit me and I crashed into the boards. I fell down and was lying on my back. I was completely winded and couldn't catch my breath. I looked up from my prone position and there were all my teammates. Except there was also a girl standing on the ice. It took me a second to realize that it was my sister Laura who was at the game and was concerned that her little brother was hurt. It took me months to shake off the taunting I got from my teammates over that. As if Plager's hit wasn't enough.

In 1975, the MPH line officially came to an end with the trade of Jimmy to the California Seals. Once the line was apart, we didn't do much as individual players. In fact, I kind of wish I'd gone with Jim to California, but it wasn't to be. Maybe someone in the Chicago management realized I wasn't happy because in the summer of 1975, rumours began to circulate about trading me. Tommy Ivan called me in that summer, just after we had traded for Joey Johnston, who had come to the team from the California in the Pappin trade.

"I want you to stay next to the phone because you've been traded," Ivan said.

I was a little surprised. "For who?"

"Well, I'm not saying because the manager of the team wants to talk with you."

I put down the phone and a half an hour later, I got a call. Johnston, the other player involved in the Chicago end of the trade, had been in a car accident the night before and they didn't know if he was going to be able to play. The trade was off, and all these years later, Ivan still won't tell me where I would have gone.

NINETEEN

The End of a Career

Perhaps because Chicago never had another player to fill Bobby's shoes, Billy Wirtz thought it would be wise to pick up Bobby Orr when he became available in 1976. Orr was the most amazing player I ever played with or against, but by the time he joined the Blackhawks he was nearing the end of his career.

His knees were about finished when he started with the team and he couldn't skate and couldn't practise. He had to know his career was near the end and I think he was pretty bitter about it. I've told him, and I mean it, that I would have given him my knees and taken his, just so I could watch him play.

The problem with Orr was that he'd go into situations that he probably never should have been in. He'd split the defenceman and plow into the boards and hurt himself. But he wouldn't have been Bobby Orr if he hadn't made those amazing moves. My brother Bobby played with Orr on Team Canada in 1976 and said Orr was the best player on the team, despite the fact he only had one leg.

At one point after he joined the Blackhawks, he didn't skate with the team for six weeks because his knees were swollen. One day he came to the stadium and said his knees felt better, so he got dressed to play and scored within the first five minutes. And he hadn't been on the ice for six weeks!

Unfortunately, Orr was just a distraction and as the team struggled, the fans decided it was time for Billy to be fired. During games they'd sing, "Good-bye Billy, Good-bye Billy" to the tune of "Good-night Ladies." Billy had a sense of humour about the whole thing, though, and even named a horse Bonjour Billy. Everything has to come to an end and there was a new way of doing things. Fitness was all the rage. There were all these machines in our dressing room. I think we used them one day and then hung our coats on them. It just wasn't the way Billy ran his team. Billy Wirtz told him we had to work on fitness. We'd do sit-ups and pushups on the ice. It was bizarre.

Billy was finally fired on Christmas Eve in 1976. On Christmas Day, we came down for a light skate because we were playing on Boxing Day. Word went around that he had been fired. I thought firing him on Christmas Eve was heartless. Later I found that they hadn't even told him in person. We had come off the road from Minnesota where we'd lost our seventh game in a row. Instead of finding him and talking to him, someone slipped a piece of paper under his door stating that he'd been fired. After practice Billy Wirtz came down to tell the team and I approached him and told him after firing Reay the way the Blackhawks did, I was quitting the team.

"That's fine," Wirtz said, "but let me tell you something. It was a mistake to fire Reay the way we did. My brother put the slip under his door when we couldn't find him. But I talked to Billy this morning and offered him the job as general manager. I wanted to make Bobby Kromm the coach. Reay told me if I was going to make him general manager, that he would name his own coach."

It was exactly the type of person Reay was. He had to have it his own way. It took a lot of guts to turn down the GM position.

I didn't want to play after they fired Billy. I was only 33, but the team wasn't going anywhere and I didn't want to go to another

team. I was a Blackhawk and couldn't imagine playing for someone else.

The team struggled after Billy left. Supposedly, after he was
fired he told Wirtz that the players on the team were his and no
other coach would have much luck with them.

"You can fire me," he said, "but none of my players will ever
be any good."

And he was right. He was the only coach I'd known from the
age of 19 and I felt lost without him. It was a strange year without
him. Bill White took over as coach, but his tenure only reinforced
the fact that Billy was a great coach. The one regret I have from
that time is that White asked me to be captain and I turned him
down. I told him I wouldn't be the captain of a bunch of losers.

In the off-season the team brought in Bob Pulford. Pulford had
been a hard-working player who wasn't overly talented. Like all
coaches who take over an older team, he just wanted to get rid
of the guys that had been hanging around. I was included in that
bunch. In many ways, that's the way the NHL is — the teams seem
to feel little responsibility for the players who played for one
team for a number of years. A lot of times they trade the older
guys. It happened to Pierre Pilote when he was dumped to
Toronto during the last year of his career.

It was clear that I wasn't going to be there long. Pulford wanted
new players that would fill the roles. I'd played every game I was
capable of playing, but the first game we were supposed to play
in 1977 was against Philadelphia and Pulford told me I wasn't
going to play. I told him that if I didn't play the first game, I
wasn't going to play any of the games.

I was hurt more than anything when Pulford told me I wasn't
going to play. When I told him I wasn't playing, he seemed kind
of happy about it, or at least he certainly didn't try to talk me out
of it. Pulford really wasn't a good communicator and I felt let
down by his attitude towards me. I'd given half my life to the
Blackhawks. Who knows what would have happened if I had
stayed on. I wanted to score 300 goals and had 298. I thought

anyone with a little compassion would have let me stay on to reach that mark. But it wasn't going to happen.

After my encounter with Pulford, I had to go see the Blackhawks' lawyer to settle my contract. The team still owed me just under a million dollars, so it was up to the management to negotiate with me. I went in to see the lawyer who was representing the team, who might just have been the most obnoxious person I've ever met. He was seated in this amazing office in downtown Chicago and immediately told me what was going to happen to me and how it was going to happen. There was no discussion with me. I listened to him for a few minutes and then told him we were going to do what I said.

"I have five more years left on a $1.5 million contract," I told him. "It's guaranteed, so I'm going to tell you what we're going to do."

"Well, we're glad to be getting rid of you," he said, as a way of explaining his behaviour. I thought his feelings towards me were a bit extreme seeing as we had never met before this occasion. It certainly wasn't a great ending to my career. I didn't want to take money for not doing anything. I just wanted to leave and not cause a problem. I was certainly not at my best, and I had these ideals which said I shouldn't take money for not doing anything. I told them I would take $100,000 and leave the team. The team's management had no problem with that arrangement.

To top it off, there was almost no concern about my disappearance from the Blackhawks lineup. I was, in a way, happy to be leaving.

Towards the middle of November, I went back to see the Blackhawks play and sat in the press box for the game. What astounded me about the game was that the top ten rows of the arena were empty. Not only was the team struggling, but for the first time since Bobby played with the team in the fifties, the fans weren't showing up.

In among these empty seats sat Ted Lindsay, the former Detroit Red Wing great who played a year with Chicago towards the end of his career. He had recently become the general manager of the Red Wings so I went over to say hello.

"I want to ask you a favour," he said. "We have a lot of young players on the Wings and it's my first year as manager. We need an experienced guy. Could you come and play for a year?"

I told Ted I'd do it, even though I really didn't want to.

There was a reason that I couldn't say no. When he first started with the Blackhawks, Bobby bought a boat and a place on Big Island in the Bay of Quinte. The boat was a Shepherd, which was very powerful and made entirely of wood. The driver always had to turn the fan on to blow the gas fumes out of the engine before turning over the ignition. One day during the summer of 1959 Bobby was taking my mother, father and grandfather out for a ride. Mom was sitting on the motor cover when Bobby turned on the engine. Only he'd forgotten to turn the blower on. When he turned the switch on, the boat blew up. The force of the explosion knocked my mother and grandfather into the water.

My grandfather Delbert used to smoke a cigar. When Bobby pulled him out of the water, he still had the cigar in his mouth. No one was killed in the explosion, but my mother was in the hospital for 16 weeks following the accident because her legs were badly burned. I was 14 at the time and I used to go to the hospital in Belleville to visit. One day I went to see her and there was a 1957 red Thunderbird convertible in the parking lot. Like any teenager, I was fascinated by the sports car because it was something I hadn't seen before. I must have looked at the car for a half hour.

When I got up to the room, there was Ted Lindsay visiting her. He'd read about the accident in the Detroit paper and had driven for six hours to come and visit her. I never forgot that visit. He'd only played with Bobby for a season at the time, but it's a clear indication of the camaraderie of the players on the Original Six teams. Bobby had liked him a lot. Bobby even named his son Blake after Ted's middle name.

If I had to do it over again, I'd have talked Ted out of getting me to play with the Wings. He was simply not getting the player he thought he was getting. I scored five goals with Detroit and had some good games, but I was really finished when my time with the Blackhawks was over. I never felt comfortable in Detroit. The team had some good players, like Terry Harper, Nick Libbet, and Dan Maloney. Reed Larson could shoot the puck harder than anyone I had ever seen, including Bobby. They were great guys, but it wasn't the same atmosphere as there had been with Chicago.

The one exception is Nedomansky. Ned had become a life-long friend. The team made the playoffs that year, the last year Detroit would make it until 1983–84, and beat Atlanta in the first round, which was a big upset, before losing to the Canadiens. Even in Detroit I couldn't beat Montreal.

The team was in the same position as Chicago: middle of the pack and lucky to make the playoffs. I had a year left on my contract with Detroit following the season, but one season had been enough. The only problem was that I was only 34 and had no idea what I would do next. My entire life had revolved around hockey.

I knew I didn't want to waste any time finding out what I was going to do. That was the worst thing about hockey — all you do is wait. You wait for the game. You wait for the plane. The game only takes a few hours to play, but you have to dedicate the rest of your day to those few hours. What are you supposed to do when you've been told that you can't do anything for fear that you'll get hurt? I would be in New York, but there was no way I could go to the theatre. It drove me crazy. I loved to play. Bobby said I loved to play more than anyone he had ever played with or against. But I hated waiting and wasn't going to be patient any longer.

While I was trying to figure out what came next, Sue approached me and asked what I thought. What I really wanted to do was work at Ridley College, a private school outside of St. Catharines, where I lived after I finished with the Blackhawks. I liked the atmosphere of the school. It had its own rink and I thought I might be able to coach, so I called the school, talked to Al Orr, the president (no relation to Bobby), and mentioned to them that I was around and was looking to work. It turned out that they had started a sports school in the summer and Orr offered me a job as the head of Sports Ridley. The school offered hockey, tennis and soccer.

I told them I would do it under one condition: I had to be allowed to teach.

"Well, have you graduated from university?" Orr asked.

I told him I hadn't.

"If you graduate from university then you'd be more than welcome to teach here." So I took the position as the head of the sport's program, although I still had a desire to teach.

Ned came to St. Catharines to help out with the camp because I knew that he had been the junior national champion of tennis in Czechoslovakia, had played a game on their national soccer team and had played on the national hockey team. Given his inclinations towards the sports we were teaching, he was a natural fit.

As part of the program to develop soccer, Ned and I were invited to play against a boys' team from Toronto which consisted of kids in their early teens. I'd never played soccer and the score was 2–1 for the Toronto team at the half.

"Dennis, are we supposed to be trying to win?" Ned asked during the break.

"Well yeah," I told him. "I'm not running up and down the field for nothing."

"ok, when we start the second half, go down the field and make sure there's a player between you and the goalie so you're not off-side."

He took the ball, went through the team and passed it to me. I kicked it into an open net. The next day I went to read the *Toronto Star* and there was a cover photo of me kicking the ball into the net. It's funny, but with my hockey career behind me, everything was working out exactly as I'd hoped.

TWENTY

Flirting with the Stars

I became determined that I was going to teach so I went to
Brock University in St. Catharines, took the test for mature
students, and passed. I was heading to university. It turned out
to be the most fun I had in my entire life. I never missed a class.

I'm of the opinion that going to university when you're older
is more fun than when you're younger. My wife would send my
son, daughter, and myself off to school at the same time. The one
thing that bothered me was that I might be treated differently.
I had been a professional hockey player, played in the Stanley
Cup and the Summit Series, and was pretty well known around
St. Catharines.

One of my first classes at Brock was a French course with a
man named Professor Rosmarin. It was my first class on my first
day back to school. The class started at 9 AM, and I sat in the
parking lot wondering if I was crazy for attempting this. But I
remembered what Billy had told me.

"It doesn't matter how you feel right now," he said, "because
in a year from now it will all be behind you. It may seem like a
big deal now, but it won't be in a few years."

So I made up my mind: I would walk into the class and three
years later I would walk out. It became clear soon after class

that Professor Rosmarin wasn't a big hockey fan. While dealing with the attendance, he came to my name on the list and
stopped.

"You're the plumber, right?" he asked. "I've got a problem with
a sink and wondered if you could take a look."

Once I started taking my degree, Ridley College let me start
teaching. During my second and third years at Brock, I would
take classes at the University and jump in my car, put on a shirt
and tie and head over to Ridley to teach. I taught Canadian
history my first year. I walked in and there were ten boys in my
first class. There had been more kids at the Hull table, so it wasn't
a big concern.

My brothers and sisters could have gone to university, but at
the time they were finishing high school, it was more common
just to get a job. My sister Jackie was the top student in all of
Belleville, never dropping below a 95 per cent average. She ended
up as the secretary to the mayor of Belleville. My sister Judy
became a nurse and she spent most of her time in the emergency
room because she liked the action. She told me once she was
disciplined after treating a patient who had broken his arm at a
McDonald's. It was during the time McDonald's was using the
"You deserve a break today" slogan and Judy told the patient that
he was being too literal with it. The patient, she said, wasn't
impressed.

My sister Laura, who passed away from breast cancer a few
years ago, worked for Loblaws. But when you have seven sisters,
you also end up with seven brother-in-laws. They were all like
brothers to me, except for Laura's alcoholic husband, who may
just have been the biggest jerk on the face of the planet.

But not all of my sisters' boyfriends seemed good when I first
met them. In 1953, Maxine started dating a man named Bill
Messer who drove a big Packard. My brothers and I were not
thrilled about Maxine dating him, so we started throwing rocks
at his car.

They've been married for 40 years now and for their anniversary, I sent him a bag of rocks. He kept them, in the bag, in the middle of his kitchen table.

Garry went back to working, and he worked on construction and as a lumberjack, among other jobs. We eventually bought a farm together, near Peterborough. We had 300 head of cattle, but I would have to leave every fall to go to training camp. Our neighbour, a man by the name of Howard Fair, saw me work all summer and then leave in the fall. It was only in the fourth year Garry and I farmed together that my fall disappearance seemed unusual to him.

"Dennis, I don't think this is reasonable," Howard said to me, just before I left.

"What do you mean?"

"Well, every time the fall comes, you go south and leave Garry with all the work."

It's only then that it dawned on me that he had no idea where I was going.

In 1970, Garry and I were working on the farm and struck up a conversation about how he had missed his chance to play pro hockey. I thought about it, called the Blackhawks and asked if he could try out. Garry was very excited and spent all summer getting into shape.

He went down to camp and did well enough to be invited to stay with one of the Blackhawks' farm teams. He thought about it, but he had four kids and the farm, so he decided against it. But at least he found out he might have made it and I think it meant a lot to him.

Ron was better at football than at hockey. He was the star halfback at Quinte High in Belleville. He was one of the best players in the country and his coach, Jack Sisson, had played for the Argonauts. Sisson wanted Ron to go to the Argos training camp, but Ron decided to get on with things. It's a funny thing, but a lot of the Hulls, my nephews included, are homebodies and never stray too far. I guess if everything's there for you, why leave?

All of my family members came to my graduation in 1980.

Even Jimmy and Pit came. I guess they thought it was unusual for a hockey player to go back to school, but it was really the only thing I could do that still allowed me to get the summers off.

ollowing my graduation I taught at Ridley, but another job drew me back to Chicago. A friend had arranged a meeting for me with the Illinois Institute of Technology, a college in Chicago. They told me they wanted me to take over as their athletic director, and I took the job because it was a new challenge.

The first time I saw Billy Wirtz after I took the job I asked him how many sports teams he was responsible for.

"Well you know, just the Blackhawks," Wirtz said.

"That's nothing," I replied, "I look after eleven."

It was a lot of fun — the kids were all architects and engineers, so the school didn't have great teams, though we were strong in baseball. At one point, every member of the women's volleyball team was on the Dean's Honour list. We took them up to play in a tournament at Brock. They not only won the tournament, but between games, they'd be studying. I also brought Brock's basketball team down to play our team. Brock's team was ranked number one in the country at the time.

"What are you doing?" the coach of the team asked. "They're number one ranked and you're bringing them down here? We're going to get killed."

"Relax," I told him, "this is Canadian basketball."

I taught at the school from 1982 until 1990, when my third career as a banquet speaker began to take too much of my time. It was getting to be unfair to ITT; I was doing a lot of these banquets and was often away. And because ITT was a private school, the money wasn't unlimited and the school began to make cuts in the late eighties.

One of my baseball coaches, Raleigh Wosniak, left in 1989 to take a job in Florida. The problem was that he didn't like the job there and wanted to come back to the school. Around the same time, our basketball coach left. I thought Raleigh would be a good coach at any sport, so I was going to bring him back as the basketball coach. He didn't have any experience though, which was a problem for some people in the school. It looked like there wasn't a way to re-hire him. Eventually I decided to quit, which allowed the baseball coach to become athletic director. That way Raleigh could come back.

I continued living in Chicago. I went back to see the staff at the school a few months after I had resigned and discovered Raleigh had rented the baseball field for use in a movie. The movie was *A League of Their Own*, the film about female professional baseball players in the 1940s. The girls spent most of the summer practising so they'd look like ball players.

Jim Daraha, the new Athletic Director, told me to come down to the field and meet some of the girls. I went to the diamond and Jim came out to greet me along with a little dark-haired girl. The girl was tiny and couldn't have been any taller than 5-foot-5.

"Do you know who this is?" he asked me, gesturing towards the girl.

"Well, I'm sorry Miss, I don't go out to movies very often and so I don't recognize you."

"Dennis, this is Madonna."

"Oh, Madonna. I'm really sorry," I said in astonishment, "but I didn't recognize you with your clothes on."

She looked at me for a moment, trying to size up the situation.

"Well, would you like me to take them off?"

"Not right here," was all I could get out.

I've always been a big believer in making something happen if you want it badly enough. In 1992 I decided it was time for a new challenge. My son John had just turned 19 and was trying to decide what he was going to do with his life. I told him he could do anything he liked. "Look, son," I said, "see this team, the Sharks? I'm going to get a job as their colour commentator."

It was just something I wanted to do. I'd watched hockey and had auditioned once for a television job in Toronto, but it had not worked out. After being away from hockey for such a long time, I wanted to get back and be a part of it.

So I found a contact for the team and called over and over again. And when I didn't hear back, I called the owner of the team. Eventually they invited me down.

I loved it in San Jose and I loved the job, but I felt the producer, Mark Stolberger, was really hard on me considering I had no experience as a colour commentator. It was harder to do than I thought it would be. The first game, which was in Vancouver, was rough. I'd been away from the game long enough that I didn't know all the players and their backgrounds. Stolberger was yelling about how he wanted to fire me right after the game finished. It went downhill from that high-point.

It was the worst situation I'd ever been in. I was trying to learn and he'd be screaming at me all the time. I never had the chance to do it under someone who could teach as opposed to scream. Dan Rusanowsky was the play-by-play guy there and he was terrific.

I remember running into Harry Neale and he'd say, "Good luck, you're going to do great."

Good luck doing what? was the question.

Perhaps it isn't surprising that I only lasted one season. My son had more luck chasing his dream. I never wanted him to be a hockey player, though when he was young he played for a while when we lived in Chicago. I think I was out of sorts about the way I'd been treated in Chicago and thought it would be better if he did something else. It turned out that he was very talented with his hands, which led him to a job with Mercedes Benz.

Eventually he decided he wanted to go to Europe and spend some time travelling. I set him up with Ned, who was coaching in Germany, and off he went.

A little while later I got a call from John. He said he had a hard time dealing with the Germans and had decided it was time to come home. I told him he should see more of the world first because this might be the last time he would have the time to do it. He decided to stay and travelled south. It was when he was in Italy that he heard about a farm that needed some assistance. He called the place and was told there had been several inquiries about the job and that it was being given out to the first applicant who could get there.

John turned up at the farm ahead of everyone else and was given the job. It turned out to be the perfect job for him and he loved working in Italy. He called home once and said he wanted to talk to me.

It was then that I noticed my son, who I couldn't get three words out of when he was 13, was speaking fluent Italian.

"What's going on here?" I asked.

"Well Dad, I like it here. I think I'm going to stay."

"Really? What are you going to do?"

"Luciana and I are going to get married," he said, referring to the youngest daughter on the farm. "Could you come over in November and be my best man?"

I went over and attended the wedding. In fact, I was the only man at the wedding who couldn't speak Italian. He now has his own olive farm with 75 acres and has restored a pile of rubble into a house. And I'm not exaggerating when I say it was a pile of rubble. It was a house where they used to keep the animals in the basement.

In the meantime, our daughter Martha has gone on to work in New York. If people can wish one thing for their kids, it should be the hope that they will love working. Both my kids do and it has served them well. Of course I know they got that love from their mother and not me. I like to play golf.

TWENTY-ONE

The Other Star in the Hull Family

By 1980, I had also started what would later become my third career: public speaking. Though the number of banquets I did picked up in the early eighties, I had been speaking at dinners and award ceremonies since I had begun playing. During the first years of my career, Blackhawks players were greatly in demand, but few of them had time to go to any of the engagements they were invited to. Fortunately I was a rookie and had time to spare. Often when a group called and asked for a player, the Blackhawks would tell them they would send Hull. Of course they didn't tell them which one. I started to enjoy speaking in public and began to work as the Master of Ceremonies at different functions.

In 1974, Chicago hosted the All-Star game and during the dinner which preceded the game, I sat between Mayor Daley and Billy Wirtz. I opened up the menu, which was beautifully done, and saw that the guest speaker was Joan Rivers and, according to the menu, I was speaking on behalf of the players.

"Billy, what's this?"

"Oh, Dennis, I forgot to tell you," was the response.

After it was over and everyone was milling about, I saw Billy Wirtz approach Joan Rivers and thank her for doing the banquet. Then he gave her a cheque for $10,000. And she hadn't even had a good night, perhaps because she wasn't that familiar with hockey, whereas I knew all the inside stories.

He turned to me afterwards.

"Thanks, Dennis."

A few minutes later I ran into Rivers.

"I don't know who the fuck you are," she said, "but I'll never appear with you again."

"Ah, you're probably right," was all I said.

It's not as if she really had to worry about it.

My speaking engagements starting picking up soon after I retired because hockey banquets needed somebody in the winter and couldn't get NHL players. I had recently retired, so I seemed a natural choice, I guess. I started doing three or four a year and the speeches were more about hockey than they are now. I enjoyed doing it and seemed to be good at getting people to laugh. To top it off, I almost always was asked to come back and speak again. Soon I was doing 15 a year. By the early nineties, I was doing over 100 engagements a year.

I think my success is due to the fact that I'm not what people expect. They expect me to be a jock and that's not the way I am when I speak.

I've done so many of these speeches now that there's almost always someone in the audience who has seen me speak. But it's not always the case.

In 1997 I spoke at the Conn Smythe Sports Celebrity Dinner at the Toronto Convention Centre. After I finished my speech, Roger Clemens, the Cy Young winner with the Blue Jays, came up and shook my hand.

"I've been to a lot of these things," he said, "but no one has been as funny as you."

I told Roger that I remembered seeing him the night he'd struck out 20 batters in 1996. But I added the media had made too much of it: Bobby and I had struck out at least that many times in a bar in Niagara Falls the night before.

As I was being escorted out, a beautiful lady approached me. She was all decked out in diamonds and was wearing a wonderful dress.

"I've don't think I've ever enjoyed anything more than that," she said.

"Thanks very much," I said. "But, I must say you look gorgeous tonight."

There was a tap on my shoulder.

"Easy, big guy. That one's mine."

It was Clemens.

I really enjoy doing banquets, but not everyone on the circuit is as fond of them as me. Don Cherry was one guy who was not keen on doing speeches, despite the way he comes off during the Coach's Corner segment of Hockey Night in Canada. Don is exactly as he seems, except he's a bit shy in a group of people. He did banquets with me, but he'd insist on going on first because he didn't want anyone to show him up. And he hated being in front of people. Even when he does Hockey Night in Canada, nobody can be in the room. They even cover up the window in the door. He wants it to seem like it's just the two of them there. Once he had made enough money to stop doing banquets, he did.

He's always been flamboyant. The Bruins were different than everyone else. The Bruins, when he coached, would have a cooler full of beer and they'd bring it into the bus after the game. We were always blown away when we saw it, because we'd always have to hide beer from our coaches. But Cherry was just one of the guys.

He was a good coach in Boston, with the guys he had. But when he didn't have those players, he didn't have the same sort of success. He tells it like it is, though, which is why people either like him or hate him.

When I started doing the banquets regularly, I noticed there would often be an auctioneer. I met one in Moose Jaw at a bonspiel and they were auctioning off the teams. I approached the guy and asked him where he learned his trade. He said there was a school in Indiana and gave me the name of the people who did the training.

I went down to take the course at a school called Ruperts and I'll tell you, it was unlike any experience I've ever had in my life. The course ran from 6:30 in the morning until 6:30 at night for 14 days, and there were more rednecks at the school than anywhere I'd ever been. I sat next to a guy who was in the Ku Klux Klan.

My classmates were the biggest men I've ever seen. I got a picture of my graduation class and I'm one of the smallest guys there. And I certainly didn't have to be concerned about anyone recognizing me. The students at the school weren't big hockey fans. The course was broken down into different segments, including portions on horses, cars, and other items. The newest segment was sports memorabilia. There was a lesson on auctioning and the instructor had a bunch of baseball cards with a few hockey cards mixed in. In the midst of all of this was one of my cards taken when I played with the Blackhawks.

The teacher had various members of the class come up to the front of the room and auction off the cards and someone auctioned off the card of me. The guy who "purchased" it was in the same row as I was.

He was looking at this card rather intently and all of a sudden he said, "We've got a guy in this class with the same name as this guy on the card!"

Then he looked at the picture a little while longer, looked over at me and exclaimed, "It's *you!*"

After that my classmates treated me like I was a star.

Learning to auction has led to several interesting experiences. I auctioned off a Harley-Davidson bike at the Conn Smythe dinner and the guy who bought it went back to his table and realized his wife would kill him for buying it.

"I'm going to pay for it," he said, "but auction it off again."

I auctioned it off again — the grand total came to $37,000 for the bike.

*W*orking at these banquets has also given me another opportunity: to learn how to play golf and play with some of the best players in the game. I've played with the likes of Jack Nicklaus and Raymond Floyd a number of times. The funny thing is, I play at about an eight handicap and I thought I was close to being a pretty solid golfer. But every once in a while I get to play with someone like Raymond and realize how far away I am from being a truly good golfer.

The real difference is that every time I putted the ball, I was surprised if it went in. Every time Floyd putted he was surprised if it *didn't* go in.

I've known Raymond for a long time. He used to live with Jimmy Pappin in Chicago. One February we were going to L.A. and Raymond was in Florida practising. Jimmy found he didn't have any clean pants to wear on the trip, so he went into Raymond's room and grabbed a pair of his slacks that seemed to fit. When he got to L.A. he went to put them on and found they were too long, so he had them shortened. When he was back he put them into Raymond's closet, not thinking about the alterations.

Raymond went to play in the Western Open soon afterwards and when he came back, Jimmy went to pick him up.

"That's the last time I get anything made in New York," Floyd said.

"Why's that?" Jimmy asked.

Floyd said he went to play the first round of the tournament and when he walked out he realised his pants were two inches too short. It was too late to do anything about it.

Jimmy said he just sat there and didn't say anything.

We used to bring Floyd down to practise with the Blackhawks and bang him around. He was raised in the Carolinas, so he'd never played any hockey and didn't skate very well, but he wanted to try. He's without doubt one of the most competitive people I've ever met.

Floyd said one time his sponsors wanted him to fly down to Texas to play golf with this hotshot and they were willing to put up the money for the two to play in a round-by-round bet. After four days, Floyd said he'd only broken even and he'd never even heard of the guy he was playing.

His sponsors were finished, so Floyd said he'd stay around and put up his own money against this local phenom. He finally made some money after an additional two days. Floyd said they were some of the toughest rounds he played. The hotshot who wanted to play Floyd turned out to be Lee Trevino.

In 1987 I was playing with Raymond at the Nabisco Bobby Orr Golf Tournament in Emerald Hills near Stouffville, Ontario. Floyd, Ben Crenshaw, and Jack Nicklaus were all playing in the tournament.

Floyd was amazing. On the sixth hole, I said, "Raymond, what club should I hit?"

"Well, Dennis, you hit a six iron last time," he said.

Although I couldn't remember what club I'd hit, Floyd could tell me exactly what I'd used *two years* after playing with me.

He also knew every tree and hole on the course. As we were going around, Raymond was talking about leaving right after and taking the Concorde from New York to Paris where he was going to go ballooning.

"It's the first vacation I've ever had," Floyd said.

"Are you crazy?" I asked. "Your first vacation? What do you call walking at the Masters? Walking the greens of Augusta isn't enough?"

I gave my speech at the dinner after the round was finished. Nicklaus was obviously anxious to catch his plane and a helicopter had landed to take him back to a nearby airstrip. There were 150 people at the dinner and Nicklaus was on the outside of the crowd. He walked across the floor towards me.

Over her features poured a ray
Of glory never to pass away,
Her eleven children she loved alone
The greatest love we've ever known!

Years over her snowy head have passed
But children came, Laura first and Peggy last,
Never, ever to be alone on earth
Of grandchildren she has no dearth!

Her children – she made us all aspire
To do our best with flair and fire,
Her oldest son known both near and far
But she thinks each of us is a star.

Thanks, thanks our worthy Mother
We love you dearly all sisters and brothers,
Your grandchildren who live in every place
They also love your sweet embrace.

So many words, so much ado
But you were always strong and true,
We get together so very few days
I only came to sing your praise.

Written to Nan in December 1984

A poem I wrote for my mother on her 80th birthday.

"Dennis, I'd give you one of my Masters trophies if you could teach me to do what you just did," Jack said, referring to my speech.

"Well, if you've got five minutes," I suggested, "then let's step into the back room and I'll show you."

I've also played at a charity tournament with Alex Trebek, the host of *Jeopardy*. He isn't a bad golfer and it was obvious that he'd had some coaching. But I didn't realise he was such a big star. I never watched *Jeopardy* much, so I wasn't prepared for what would happen when we started. It turned out he was hugely popular, especially with the older ladies who paid special attention to him whenever we'd walk by.

Floyd must feel the same way about playing in these celebrity tournaments as I do about playing celebrity hockey games. For a while I played against a team called the Hollywood All-Stars, which consisted of actors such as Michael Keaton and Michael J. Fox.

It was funny playing hockey against these guys because some of them thought they were pretty good. Michael J. Fox got a bunch of goals one game and thought he'd done really well.

"But Michael, we let you get those goals," I said. "You're only five-foot-four for God's sake. My wife is bigger than you."

That slowed him down pretty quickly.

The coach of the Hollywood team was the actor who played Odd-Job in the James Bond movie *Goldfinger*. We went out for dinner after a game and the wine flowed freely. Eventually I started to get on Odd-Job's case a bit.

"How could you cheat that way?" I said, referring to the golf game in the movie. "How could you cheat with Goldfinger's ball?"

"But Dennis," he said, getting upset, "the director made me do it!"

*R*ecently I spoke at a golf tournament run by Wayne Gretzky's dad, Walter. Walter had an aneurism in the early nineties and he now runs a tournament to raise money for the hospital in Hamilton, Ontario, that treated him.

Before the speech, Walter told me that he had lost his memory and couldn't remember things from 1970 until 1990. He was starting to gain some of his memory back, but there was still a 20-year period he couldn't recall.

Wayne and Walter were sitting down front and I started my speech.

"It's great to be here with the greatest hockey player who has ever lived," I said. "But it's unfortunate, due to memory loss, that you can't remember 1973, Walter. That's the year I scored 60 goals."

"I might not remember," Walter yelled from the audience, "but I'm not stupid."

TWENTY-TWO

And Brett Said to Bobby

I was surprised when my nephew Brett started to make a name for himself. Because the Hull family is so large, he was simply another one of the dozens of nephews I had. I never saw him play because he lived in Vancouver, though I heard a lot about him in the draft year. I was working in Chicago at the time and sat in the press box during the draft because Jimmy Pappin was working for the Blackhawks. Bob Pulford, who was the Blackhawks' general manager, was there, too.

"Are you going to draft Brett?" I asked.

"Naw, he can't play in the NHL. He's too slow," Pulford said.

I thought Pulford knew better than I did and let it drop.

A few years later the Blues were playing the Blackhawks and I was in Chicago to watch the game. Brett got two goals and an assist, leading the Blues to a 3–1 win.

I was sitting next to Pulford and mid-way through the third period I looked at him.

"Hey Bob, it's too bad he can't skate, isn't it?"

I think sometimes they overscout and overanalyze the draft choices. The situation with Brett was similar to Doug Gilmour's draft year. I attended the draft the year after he'd broken

Gretzky's Junior scoring record. I said to Pulford that I thought Gilmour would turn into a star.

"Naw, too small to play in the NHL," was the reply.

Gilmour was chosen way down in the draft, which leads me to believe that many scouts can't judge talent. I won't say I'm a good judge of players, but I do like to watch them play.

The first time I saw Brett play was in Calgary, where I was doing a banquet. He scored three goals. The next night he didn't play in the game, though I turned up to watch. Terry Crisp, the coach, didn't dress him. Crisp told me it made Brett mad and that he'd play better after sitting.

"I don't know if it makes *him* mad," I told Crisp, "but it's sure pissing off his uncle."

I don't think Brett has suffered from the comparison to Bobby as much as I did because they play in different eras. In many ways I think *Brett's* stardom set *Bobby* back at the start. He attends lots of Brett's games and is often approached by fans when they are heading out of the arena.

"You're Brett Hull's father?" they ask, seemingly oblivious to the fact that Bobby is one of hockey's all-time greats. It's not a case of Brett having to get used to being compared to Bobby, but Bobby getting used to being the father of Brett.

*D*espite his stardom, my brother didn't change a bit from the time he left Point Anne. He treated everyone in the same fashion. He took time to make sure people got what they wanted. He'd talked to people for hours after games. The rest of us would want to be leaving for dinner and some thought it was an imposition, but Bobby never saw it that way. It wasn't even part of the job — it was just the way he was.

Bobby's wig has become famous in itself. It all stems back to the fact that, by the late 1960s, he'd lost most of his hair. He had a number of opportunities to do endorsements, but the marketing people weren't pleased.

"You're supposed to be the Golden Jet," they said, "but you don't have any hair."

He takes the wig off all the time when people aren't around. I regularly play in a golf tournament in Vancouver and after it's over, we'll head back to the hotel. For three years in a row, Bobby has given me the nod and we go into another room and Bobby puts his hair piece on me. Eddie Shack just goes berserk.

Sally, the wife of former Leaf star Bobby Baun, was at the hotel the last time I put the hair on. She wears thick glasses and doesn't see all that well. I had my brother's hair on when I went over to talk to her.

The next morning, Eddie was having breakfast with the Bauns.

"What did you think of Dennis with Bobby's hair on?" Shack asked.

"That wasn't Dennis," Sally said.

"Oh, but it definitely was Dennis."

"No, it had to be Bobby," she said, "because he came up to me and said, 'Want to come up to my room afterwards, Sally?'"

Bobby has been married three times. His first marriage was when he was in Junior, and he married a girl named Judy Leary. Because of his marriages, Bobby has a lot of kids all over the place. It's a funny thing though, because he's never seen the boy he had with Judy. I think Bobby doesn't really think the boy is his son. But I've seen a picture of him and he looks like a Hull.

Bobby's kids show up at the strangest times. The year after I retired, Bobby was playing for Hartford in a game against the Sabres in Buffalo. We were in the dressing room after the game and he called me over.

"Take a look at this," he said, pointing to a letter.

It was from a girl who had grown up with an Italian family from Buffalo. When she was 12 or 13, she had wondered why the rest of her family had dark complexions, while she had blonde hair. Soon afterwards, her family told her she had been adopted.

Many years later she found her birth-mother in St. Catharines. The mother was a baton-twirling dancer, but she refused to tell the girl who her father was. So the girl camped on the lawn until her mother would give her a name.

Eventually the girl's mother said the father was Bobby. By this time the girl was 30 and sat down and wrote Bobby the letter. It turns out she was at the Sabres game.

"Go out there and see if you can see anyone who looks like us," Bobby said to me.

I walked out and it was very crowded, but there was a girl who looked like one of my nieces. I continued to walk in her direction.

All of a sudden she saw me.

"Uncle Dennis!" I was struck by the fact she'd never seen me before, but knew who I was right off.

That year she came to the Hull family reunion — just another part of the family. My mother, who had 40 grandchildren and took great pride in knowing all of their birthdays, was sitting with me when the girl, named Beth, came up.

"Dennis, I think I'm losing it," my mother said. She was almost 80 at the time. "I can't remember that girl's name."

"For good reason, Mom," I said.

At Mom's 80th birthday, Bobby pulled another stunt. There was a big gathering for her in Belleville and I was sitting between Mom and Dad. When Bobby finally arrived, he introduced his new wife, whom no one had ever met before.

"This is Debbie," Bobby said.

"Lena, that's not my son," Dad said to Mom in a gruff, angry tone. My father said the same thing to my mother when we did something good or bad. Only the tone would change and it was clear that he was angry.

He was really upset that Bobby had screwed up my mother's 80th birthday. My mother leaned over to me and, out of earshot of my dad, said, "He's got it all wrong. That's his only son!"

As we were getting ready for the family picture, Debbie didn't feel she should be part of it. After all, she'd just met the family and didn't know us. And there are a lot of Hulls. But Mom wouldn't have any part of it.

"Come on dear," Mom said to Debbie. "We don't know how long you're going to be here."

But Bobby is still with Debbie — they've been married for 12 years.

Bobby's most recent notoriety stems from the fact that he's developed a reputation for having too good a time. When he does banquets, he realizes that for someone in Moose Jaw, Saskatchewan, meeting Bobby Hull and having a few drinks with him is a big deal. And he thinks they should be able to see him as long as they want. It hurts him physically because he often stays out all night. It may be a big night out for his fans, but Bobby never seems to realize that he has to do it 100 more times in the year. He just wants to give something back to the people.

The main thing that's changed with Bobby is his attitude towards hockey. I think he has the right to be a little bitter. He did a great deal to change hockey and hockey's never really given anything back to him. It would be great if someone gave him the chance to be in a public relations position because then he could finally have a normal lifestyle.

I know other players have had a hard time adjusting after their playing days are over. Bobby Orr, when he finished playing hockey, was at loose ends because of Eagleson and was searching for a new career. When he got hired by Nabisco, he changed his life and took some PR classes. He now works representing players.

I think an opportunity like Orr's would work wonders for Bobby. He's always been — and I know it's an overworked term — a "loose cannon," and Brett's now got the same reputation. But Bobby wasn't like that when he played. He had respect for the game and for Billy Reay and he's tremendously disappointed about the way players today act towards the fans. Hockey players always had the reputation for being nice to the fans and reporters, but now they're getting the same reputation as baseball players, which is disappointing as far as Bobby is concerned.

He's also had a lot to say about the whole Alan Eagleson affair. The more I think about how things went, the more I'm disappointed, but Bobby is angry. I just can't believe that a person like Eagleson, who has so much power, could abuse his position. Hockey players were easy targets because, at the time, most didn't know anything about contracts or pensions. We were focused on the game. We trusted Eagleson to look after things. He had a $1 million contract. How much did he need? Taking $15,000 from a player's insurance; that's just greed.

If he had considered it, he would have been the commissioner of the NHL. The owners loved him because he kept salaries down and would have put him in that position.

And I can't really blame Billy Wirtz for his involvement with Eagleson. He obviously thought it was good for business and his business came first. It did seem odd for Eagleson to be a friend of a number of owners and a players' agent at the same time. But we just didn't consider the possibility that he could be ripping us off. Pensions were never foremost in our minds. Eagleson approached us after practice, when the players wanted to be elsewhere, and said we'd have to put in $1,500 a year and the owners would match it. At the end of our careers, there would be $1,000 a year for each year we played. All I thought was that if I played for 15 years, I would make $15,000 a year after I retired for doing nothing. It sounded like a lot of money. No one thought about inflation. Then to find out that the owners were getting their $1,500 from the interest on our $1,500 was a real blow.

But you never hear Frank Mahovlich or Jean Béliveau speak out as much as Bobby. They're more community-oriented. Bobby can't even sit back now and enjoy himself — he still has to work. It's generally because of situations he put himself in in the past, but I wish he could just farm and take it easy. It would be good for him.

*A*s professional hockey has drifted away from Bobby, Bobby has also ceased to be as involved with the game. A few years ago we found each other in Chicago and Bobby mentioned he wanted to go to a game. Even though he's Bobby Hull, a legend in Chicago, he was worried about getting into Chicago. Of course there's no one in the city who doesn't know him, but he insisted I call ahead to make sure we could get in. I tried to tell him there wouldn't be a problem and that I had simply shown up on numerous occasions.

When we got there tickets were waiting.

"Bobby, let's go sit in the press box," I said.

"C'mon. There's no way we can get in there," he said.

"I get in on my own. There's no way they're going to turn you away. Let's go."

We headed up to the press box and there was a guard there who immediately recognized Bobby. When we walked into the press box, which is right over the net, someone must have seen him, because pretty soon everyone in the stands knew he was there. It travelled around the arena. As Bobby was saying hello to the people in the box, 18,000 fans stood and began cheering. Bobby was oblivious to it and continued to say hello to those around him. Meanwhile the play on the ice had stopped.

"Hey Dennis, what's going on out there," he asked. "Did someone score?"

"No, Bobby. They're cheering for you."

TWENTY-THREE

You're Not Dennis Hull!

My dad died in 1993, a short while after my mother passed away. He didn't cope very well without her; they were a close couple and didn't have many friends.

He always talked a good game, right up until the end. Dad always said he was a hockey player in the summer and a baseball player in the winter. His big thing when we were growing up was to tell us we couldn't make it.

"You guys will never play in the NHL," he said, "you're living a pipe dream."

He said it all the time, even when we were playing.

"You guys are finished. They'll have you out of there by Christmas. You're no goddamn good."

In fact, it took over twenty years to get the whole family together again for Christmas. During the Christmas of 1981, after Bobby and I retired, we all reunited.

On Christmas Eve, Bobby and I arrived at the same time. We walked in together and Dad was sitting at the kitchen table. I had played 14 seasons in the NHL and Bobby had played over 20. We had both been successful and played in numerous Stanley Cups. With both of us standing there, Dad decided he had to have the last word.

"I told you two that you'd never make it," he said.

$\mathcal{E}$very once in a while you meet people who change and influence your life. Like Bobby and Billy, or Pit Martin and Jimmy Pappin, there are certain people who have a lasting impact on the way my life has turned out. I've been very fortunate to meet those people, while my other brothers, who also wanted to be hockey players, didn't encounter the people who might have changed their lives.

Most recently I've met Ron Joyce, one of the founders of Tim Horton's, the donut empire. He's a special guy — lots of people have lots of money, but I've never met anyone like him who uses their money to help other people. He sends thousands of kids to camp every year, and he doesn't have to. He could simply buy an island in the South Pacific and nobody would notice. Except the underprivileged kids he sends to camp every year.

I did the first Tim Horton's fundraiser about seven years ago because I was doing well and wanted to do something for other people. There's certainly a lot of charities that are deserving, but there was something about the Tim Horton's charity that made it special.

I'd done the banquets without a fee for a number of years, but Ron always wanted to give me something for doing them. In 1987, Ron told me he wanted me to do all my banquets for the kids' camps. People now pay my fee directly to the camp.

Ron is a lot like Bobby. I didn't know him before when he was a policeman, but I can't believe he was any different than he is now. He never wants to be the centre of attention. When I'm with him, he wants to make me the focus of everything.

"Tell him that story, Dennis," he says, whenever we're out with people.

He also can stay up late just like Bobby. At one of the kids' camps there was a golf tournament and I brought Bobby along.

After the tournament, Ron served 1,000 lobsters. The first one he ate must have weighed ten pounds. Then he ate two more, all the while drinking wine, before moving onto whiskey. Eventually Bobby asked me to take him back to Ron's house where we were staying. I remember Bobby locking the door, which I thought was pretty odd, because Bobby likes a late party.

Two hours later, the party was over and Ron came back and knocked on Bobby's door.

"Come on Bobby," he said, "get up."

Then I realized why Bobby had locked the door — he'd finally met his match.

The next morning, I got up at 8 AM and Ron had already gotten up and left.

I must admit there isn't much left that I want to do that I haven't already done. My wife calls it a four-letter "F" word, but I must admit there's a part of me that wants to go back to farming. I always liked working on farms as a kid, and then I worked on Bobby's farm. It's sort of like hockey — it's hard to get out of your blood.

Recently Sue thought I bought a farm and kept accusing me of doing the dastardly deed. She thought I was going to reveal it on Christmas. Instead I gave her earrings with farm animals on them. She told me the earrings had better be the only farm animals she gets close to.

I now do 100 banquets a year, which is the most I can do. Despite the fact that I've spoken to thousands of people and had three successful careers, every so often something brings me back to earth.

A few years ago I was in Saskatoon the day after I'd done a banquet. I was in a men's washroom doing my business at a urinal, and this other fellow in the washroom kept looking over at me. I assumed that he knew who I was, so I didn't pay too much attention and when I finished I went to wash my hands. After I was done, the fellow, who was still watching me, walked over. I decided to introduce myself.

"I noticed you recognize me, I'm Dennis Hull," I said, holding out my hand.

He shook it.

"It's a pleasure to meet you, I'm Gordie Howe," he said.

I've known what Gordie Howe looks like since I was a kid. This wasn't Mr. Hockey.

"You're not Gordie Howe."

"Well, if you can say you're Dennis Hull," he said, "I can say I'm Gordie Howe."

With that he turned and walked out of the washroom.